RADICAL HUMILITY

ESSAYS ON ORDINARY ACTS

RADICAL HUMILITY

ESSAYS ON ORDINARY ACTS

EDITED BY

REBEKAH MODRAK

AND

JAMIE VANDER BROEK

Belt Publishing

Printed in the United States of America
First edition 2021
1 2 3 4 5 6 7 8 9

ISBN: 978-1-948742-96-2

Belt Publishing
5322 Fleet Avenue
Cleveland, Ohio 44105
www.beltpublishing.com

Cover by Ben Denzer
Book design by Meredith Pangrace
Illustrations by Nick Tobier

*To Ottilie, Lucy, and Oscar, with our hope
for the future.*

Radical humility ...

AN INTRODUCTION

Sarah Buss

This collection began with the summer residency featured in the first essay. In July 2016 Rebekah Modrak left behind a world permeated with the value of self-promotion, to live among people whose habits of mind and deed directed their attention—and the attention of others—away from themselves. There, in Aurora, Nebraska, she observed humility as a way of life.

What, exactly, did she observe? The essays that follow are a response to Modrak's decision to invite people from a wide range of backgrounds to reflect on the nature and value of humility. Perhaps more importantly, most of these reflections describe specific contexts in which humility has played a key role. These contexts include hospitals, universities, and libraries; restaurants and restaurant kitchens; makers' spaces and the spaces where athletes compete. They include friendships and the relationships between the frail and the healthy.

The variety of styles and the many different perspectives represented in these essays provide us with an antidote to any temptation we may have to make easy generalizations about the issues they address. Nonetheless, several themes emerge. In this introduction, I will call attention to a few of these themes, hoping that the readers will treat my brief observations as a prompt to draw their own connections and raise their own questions.

Humility is commonly contrasted with arrogance and pride. Arrogance is clearly a vice: the vice of assuming that one is superior to, and more important than, others. But what about pride? We encourage our children to be proud of themselves; defenders of equal rights often march under the banner of "pride." In short, as several of the essays suggest, though a person cannot be both arrogant and humble, there is an important sense in which someone can be proud and humble at the same time.

This point is closely related to another: humility is not servility. To refrain from regarding oneself as superior to others is not to regard oneself as inferior. As Aaron Ahuvia and Jeremy Wood note, hierarchical societies value this deferential stance—at least in those who are at a lower level in the hierarchy. But we no longer see things this way. We do not think that this sort of deference is compatible with self-respect. It is widely assumed that if we value ourselves properly, we will interact with one another as equals.

This having been said, it would be a mistake to conclude that the disposition to defer to others is no longer one of the things we value in valuing humility. As several of the essays in this collection stress, to be humble is to appreciate one's fallibility. It is to know how little one knows. Indeed, as Troy Jollimore and Charles M. Blow remind us, humility involves acknowledging that some people are one's superiors in knowledge, given their experience and training. And it involves being disposed to learn what one can from these people. To be humble is to appreciate that when one disagrees with someone, it may not be this other person who is confused and mistaken. We need not deny that all people are created equal in order to concede that some people's opinions have more to be said for them than others.

I mentioned experience as well as training. A humble person is not only prepared to learn from those with greater expertise. She is also deeply aware of how much can be gained by engaging nonexperts with an open mind and heart. As both Jollimore and Agnes Callard explain, it was this awareness that drove Socrates to seek out others in his quest for wisdom. In different ways, Eranda Jayawickreme and Melissa Koenig and Valerie Tiberius also call our attention to what we miss, and what significant benefits we forego—whether in business or in personal relations—when we presume to know more than the people with whom we interact. Koenig and Tiberius draw a further connection between being open to learning from others and being less prone to treating them in ways that do more harm than good. When, for example, we do not seriously account for the fact that someone's cares and concerns may be very different (and no less important) than our own, even our benevolent impulses can have harmful effects on those we are trying to help.

Of course, sometimes other people need to learn from *us*. And having the courage of one's convictions is just as important as being prepared to modify one's convictions in response to one's interactions with others. The philosopher Friedrich Nietzsche points out that few great deeds would be done, and few great works of art would be created, if people never closed their minds to the many reasons they have for questioning the value of what they are doing. Rick Boothman illustrates this point with his story of how—in the face of powerful opposition—he quit his job as a lawyer defending hospitals against malpractice suits, convincing a major hospital system to incorporate greater humility into the practice of medicine.

And Callard stresses the need to combine humility with self-confidence when she notes that the person who is eager to learn from others must rely on the fact that these others have confidence in their own beliefs. In order to expand our knowledge, we must start somewhere. A situation in which everyone suspends her judgments about everything is at least as bad as a situation in which everyone is confident that she has no reason to question her convictions.

Though, as Koenig and Tiberius stress, many of our mistakes reflect the fact that we lack adequate concern for the perspectives of others, our failures can yield lessons in humility even when they cannot be attributed to any such insensitivity. When we fail to achieve our goals, we are often prompted to reconsider how our interests and concerns relate to the interests and concerns of others. In his essay Mickey Duzyj recounts the trajectories of athletes whose public failures—and even humiliations—prompted them to reject their self-involved ambitions and devote themselves to improving the lives of others. As many studies have shown, people who thus redirect their attention and efforts usually end up living far more fulfilling lives as a result.

The connection between being less self-absorbed, on the one hand, and being more generous, on the other, is the theme of Ruth Nicole Brown's homage to her remarkable Aunt Dottie. Ami Walsh, Kevin Hamilton, Lynette Clemetson, and Jamie Vander Broek each also stress the extent to which a humble person—and as Vander Broek notes, a humble *institution*—will move into the background in order to enable others to move into the foreground. More particularly, Walsh and Clemetson highlight the humility involved in encouraging people to tell their own stories. And Vander Broek and Hamilton stress the value of supporting the efforts and inquiries of others in ways that involve helping them to follow their own lead.

In effect, this is another respect in which humility involves deference. The same point is central to Gilbert Rodman's discussion of the way that a just copyright law would facilitate the recognition of artistic contributions that are too often left in the background. In speaking of the indignities of aging, Russell Belk also reminds us how easy it is to treat certain people as unworthy of respect and concern. If, he claims, we are to avoid contributing to the humiliations of those who are old and sick, we must cultivate the qualities identified with humility. This involves, among other things, not privileging the perspective of those who are young and healthy—not treating this perspective as more authoritative, more worthy of being taken seriously and accommodated.

Not only can a humbling experience have a valuable effect; it can also be valuable in itself. This is possible, at any rate, if one's identity is not tied up with impressing others with one's knowledge or talents or skills. In short, if one is truly humble, then failure—even public failure—need not be a blow to one's self-esteem. For this reason, a humble person can adopt a less defensive posture in her relation to others—and even a more playful attitude toward her attempts to realize her goals. Nadia Danienta and Aric Rindfleisch illustrate this point in discussing people who experiment with 3D printing, and who delight in their failures as well as their successes. Humility, these people teach us, is freeing.

Failure is not the only spur to humility. Gaining a deeper appreciation of the fact that we are just one among many can be as simple as appreciating how connected we are to others. To incorporate the sense of oneself as part of a complex web of mutual dependence is to become more humble. At the same time, this humility enhances one's ability to form bonds with others. In short, retreating from the center of things—both in reality and in one's self-conception—is inseparable from forging connections that expand the boundaries of one's self. Several essays in the collection allude to this phenomenon in one way or another. (See, especially, the essays by Jennifer Cole Wright and Ruth Nicole Brown.)

In 1950 a Gallup Poll asked U.S. high school students the question: "Do you think you are an important person?" Only 12 percent of respondents said yes. When the same question was posed in 2006, more than 80 percent said "yes." This dramatic shift corresponded to a dramatic increase in the value U.S. educators attributed to cultivating self-esteem. These trends raise many questions. Here I will simply note that there is ample evidence that the increase in self-esteem has corresponded to a decrease in humility. The greater tendency to think well of oneself has corresponded to the tendency to think more of—and about—oneself than one thinks of—and about—anyone else.

In her essay Wright offers us a compelling description of what has been lost: not only the benefits that humility confers on us, but also—and more importantly—the distinctive benefit that consists of relating to oneself and the world with humility. In the poem near the end of the collection, Tyler Denmead wonders whether, given his privilege as a white man, he can possibly realize this ideal. Is it really possible to de-center oneself so radically? In seeking an answer to this question, we might start by turning to the last essay in the collection: Kevin Em's brief account of his transition from the tech world to the world of the restaurant (and then hospital) kitchen. Like Modrak's summer journeys to Nebraska, this was a transition to a place of greater humility. It was occasioned by Em's failure to achieve his earlier professional goals. And it was made possible by new connections and dependences, which were, in turn, strengthened by the humility they inspired. Em offers us a portrait of what it is like to be less visible to others, even as one is more attuned to their needs and desires. He describes the greater freedom and generosity that accompany these other changes, and the pride he feels in relating to himself and others in this way. Together with the other essays, this final story prompts us to ask: how might we combine these ingredients in our own lives?

as a new way of
being in the world

FREE YOURSELF BY CHOOSING THE PLAIN CRACKERS

Rebekah Modrak

I left Ann Arbor to spend five weeks in the small town of Aurora, Nebraska, happily fleeing an increasingly self-absorbed university culture that seemed to be remaking itself to conform to a corporate model.

My work as an art professor had meant playing in the garden of revelation. For many years, the voices of my advisors and colleagues spoke of meaning. Tell us what you learned from making that artwork? What ideas are you exploring? Why are they significant? How are they connected to the world? Dean Bryan Rogers would refer to us as "creative critters," as though we fiercely sniffed out our environments with curious snouts. "Get into trouble," he'd say.

And then he retired and, suddenly, the word from on high spoke "visibility." My first encounter with the question—"How are you visible?"—baffled me to the point of almost answering, "Can't you see me? I'm right here beside you." Are you making yourself visible? How can you become more visible? These new questions encouraged us to think of ourselves as branded commodities and compelled us to incessantly self-monitor. We were learning to be shining examples of what Andrew Ross refers to as the convergence of academics and entrepreneurial cultures.

We had a new Visibility Committee.

We stopped exhibiting paintings and prints in the public, informal spaces of our art building (too messy and "uncurated") and, instead, administrators commissioned mural-sized photos of professors, posed in the act of working, with any actual artworks as background. Cursory questions caption each image, cementing our affiliation with entrepreneurial buzzwords like "community," and asserting the usefulness of art and design to "improve the quality of our lives." We artists are now branded as leaders driving relevant, urgent "creative research." If critic Bill Deresiewicz were to witness this display, he might ruefully comment that, "Things have value in the market insofar as they are useful." In the self-promotion ethos, I am no longer Rebekah. I'm a walking monitor of self-projection laden with the baggage of others' insecurities.

To be clear, I'm in favor of the idea that people, and/or their work, should be seen, heard, understood, and celebrated. We shouldn't work in isolation. We should think about context and distribution. But now, visibility alone seems to be the guiding factor. Colleagues presenting to the faculty for review no longer describe their work process, their ideas, their discoveries, and their challenges. They list conferences or titles of exhibitions and papers. They show images of themselves giving talks without describing the substance of the talk. Our school hosts "boaster" sessions with other schools, mixers that begin with a round of one-minute introductions, conducive to declarative statements about our own importance.

The atmosphere changed from frolicking to fear. Some creatures, even creative critters, respond to fear with behavior meant to make our animal selves appear larger than we really are. In the animal world, it's called threat display. We were becoming Australian lizards fanning the frills on either side of our heads. Since some feel more visible when they can make others less so, this leads to other perversions, to bullying, belittling, and abuse of power.

With support from a university grant, I put this culture in my rear-view mirror that June and headed to Nebraska with my family to ask farmers about their labor. Our destination: a five-week residency on a farm. The series of interviews had started in Michigan and grew out of my artwork *Re Made Co.*, which presents as an online artisanal plunger company to parody actual company Best Made Co.'s $350 striped bespoke axes, titled with names like the Black Donald American Felling Axe. Wealthy New Yorkers hang these fetishes over their mantels, as if to make visible a connection with manual labor. When Best Made's attorneys sent me a cease and desist saying that I was stealing "their work," it seemed only logical to recreate the legal document from the perspective of workers with the legitimate right to own manual labor.

I listened to carpenters, custodians, construction workers, landscapers, and farmers, mostly surprised at being asked to talk about their work, accustomed to people caring about the products of their labor rather than the laborer, but willing to put their work into words. At Grain Place Farms in Aurora, Mike Herman told me:

> Nobody's ever asked me about physical labor before. It was just a given. That's what you did. What do you discuss about physical labor? So that just kind of threw me for a little bit there and I go, okay, I'm not sure where this is going but we'll find out.

When folks in Aurora heard I was interviewing farmers, several said: "Talk to farmer Ned." "Ned's the best farmer. Make sure you talk with him." At the third recommendation, I asked, "What makes Ned such a good farmer?" Does he know special methods for crop rotation? Does he have innovative methods of pest control?

"He's humble."

Humble.

Humble.

A word I had never heard discussed at my university.

Farmers think in year-long increments, through 365 days of preparation, planting, cultivating, and harvesting, but weather has the final say in any plan. Every farmer had a story.

Mim who started the Country Lavender Farm:

I planted three thousand lavender plants by hand, weeded, trimmed, and harvested by hand. Then the winter kill two thousand plants. Anything that survived the winter kill had their leaves sucked off by a tornado.

Mike at Grain Place:

Last year we got hailed out. Lost all the barley. The corn and the popcorn was at such a stage that it would come back, was young enough. I had to replant all my soybeans.

I asked Mike, "How long did it hail?"

Minutes. You're talking frozen water falling from the sky and you add a little wind with that, and it'll just shear everything off. The corn, which was four- to six-leaf stage, was just a little nubbins out there.

The best farmer is adaptive. She knows that any of a hundred variables is more powerful than herself. She accepts that and adapts. She's contemplating three options or directions before the hailstones stop falling.

My family and I stayed at an art residency on a former farm, in a grain elevator, perched atop an old two-story barn. We showed up at every town barbeque and pancake breakfast advertised in the *Aurora News Register*. Eating BBQ pork sandwiches in the Aurora town square, we chatted with the husband and wife who sat at our picnic table. They asked us about the residency, told us stories about local history, and, when he left to talk with neighbors and we asked more questions, the woman shyly mentioned that her husband was the mayor.

At a pancake and sausage breakfast hosted by the Aurora Municipal Airport the following weekend, we watched circles of batter squirt onto the griddle by the dozens and listened to a father tell us sweet stories about his son's cycling adventures. He headed out and a farmer leaned over and whispered, "That's one of our state senators." Everybody seemed willing to leave the room without our knowing their title, rank, and status, that is, without being visible.

I don't claim rural Nebraska as the center of virtuous behavior. In running one of the few organic farms in the area, farmer Mike has to reckon with pesticide drift from neighboring conventional farms that strip their own soil of nutrients and poison the land with fertilizer and solvents, even as they co-opt the language of ecology. In his words:

> There's a lot of conventional farmers associating themselves with sustainable activity. They've changed the definition of what sustainable is to meet their needs. So, therefore, what's important in the sustainable aspect is that they continue to do what they're doing. It's sustainable. Whereas, in our definition, it's sustaining the Earth, the big picture. Not the little picture.

There's much to say for the life we live when visibility isn't a main concern, when you can leave a room without disclosing anything about yourself, when you can accept yourself as an ordinary, adaptable figure in the midst of more powerful, indiscriminate forces.

Being in Aurora, Nebraska returned me to the obliviousness to status that defined the first thirty years of my life. Growing up in Pittsburgh, having exactly what we needed and no more was a financial reality but also a personal and political stance. The first payment for the house we moved into when I was four left no money for lightbulbs and we lived by the house's available light for several weeks. We had no tv, few possessions, and sparse used furnishings. *Exactly what we needed and no more* is why I still remember the Hostess chocolate cupcake with vanilla swirls that my mother bought my sister and me from the hardware store on the corner, on a swelteringly hot day, as we waited for a bus that never seemed to come. It's why I remember the conversation about snobbism my father had with me midway through my fifth grade year, after some friends started to talk about Chic jeans, then to wear Chic jeans, and I reluctantly and shamefully brought up the question to my parents. In truth, even the idea of the jeans was a burden—a smokescreen in a world otherwise fully occupied by things that mattered: play, work, music, people, and relationships. It was a relief to have that first flame of visibility and status deftly extinguished by my parents, to recoup from this social tornado and find new friends who didn't think to talk about jeans.

There's something to be said for being pleased with the choice of four kinds of crackers at the Aurora Mall, the family-run business that serves as grocery, hardware, toy, and office supply store in Aurora, Nebraska. Ritz crackers, Triscuits, graham crackers, or NutThins.

In Ann Arbor, we have Cauliflower Crackers (sea salt, nacho, and cheddar), Butternut Squash Crackers (sea salt, parmesan), Grain-Free (sea salt, everything, and pizza), Sweet

Butter Crackers, Crispy Cornbread Crackers, Flatbread Crisps, Brown Rice Snaps (unsalted, toasted onion, vegetable, and black sesame), Savory Rice Thins, Melba Toasts (whole wheat, sesame, classic), Buckwheat Crispbreads, Chestnut Crispbreads, Quinoa Crispbreads, Rosemary Sourdough Crackers, Carr's Crackers (water, cheese melts, whole wheat, and cracked pepper), Stone Wheat, Briton Crackers, Cabaret Crisp and Buttery Crackers, Bruschettini (cracker pepper, garlic and parsley, black and green olives, and rosemary and olive oil), Moon Cheese Crackers, Parmesan Cheese Crisps, Asiago and Pepper Jack Cheese Crisps, Ak-Mat Crackers, Aged Cheddar Beer Crackers, Oyster Crackers, Wasa (whole grain, multi-grain, and crisp-n-light), and RyVita Sesame Rye Crispbread.

Six by ten feet of crackers. In one store.

Ann Arbor excesses had inched up on me, made possible— for the first time in forty years—by the unfamiliar presence of disposable income. The first time I shopped for food in Aurora, I thought "there's nothing here." No organic grapes, local yogurt, wild-caught salmon, or real bagels. Within weeks, I came to love the ease of shopping in Aurora, grabbing the NutThins and spending no more time than that wondering what kind of cracker would be just right for me. The store said, "This is what we have. You can be happy with this." I felt lighter.

I dreaded returning home to the aisle of spelt, crisp bread, and cracked pepper crackers and the arms race of status directing us to external meaning and increasingly rarified objects. I listened to a rancher describe fighting the Keystone pipeline, drank dandelion wine with new friends, and walked through a restored prairie with fantastically large cow pies. I felt true joy from the sensation of the cool public pool water calming the chigger bites on my legs. And I exited a lot of rooms without caring whether or not I was visible.

ESCAPING THE GRAVITATIONAL PULL OF THE SELF

Jennifer Cole Wright

Everything in my own immediate experience supports my deep belief that I am the absolute center of the universe; the realest, most vivid and important person in existence. We rarely think about this sort of natural, basic self-centeredness...it is our default setting, hard-wired into our boards at birth.

—David Foster Wallace

As David Foster Wallace rightly noted in a celebrated 2005 commencement speech at Kenyon College, each of us experiences ourselves as standing, psychologically speaking, at the center of a universe. That is to say, we each experience ourselves as the "organizing center" of a consciousness that feels woven together into the form of a life. *Our* life.

We experience that life as real and substantial, as something to be lived, equipped with the drive to fulfill basic needs and to pursue goals and values that we experience as worthwhile and meaningful. It seems only natural, then, that in a world filled with needs and desires, it is *our own* needs and desires that press most strongly in upon us, demanding our attention. And in a world filled with beliefs, values, goals, and ideals, it is *our own* that strike us as the most attractive and compelling, the most true and worthy of commitment and pursuit.

It is not simply a matter of our needs, desires, beliefs, values, goals, and ideals (hereafter, "needs, etc.") being the ones with which we happen to be most intimately and continuously familiar, but rather the fact that they emanate from our center—we experience them as *ours*—and, in so doing, they generate a powerful gravitational pull.

This pull typically manifests as a self "centered-ness" (i.e., a self-oriented focus) through which we privilege and prioritize our needs, etc. above those of others. They are the ones we attend the most to: we expend more energy on them, we give them more thought, we dedicate more resources to them, and we allocate to them more time.

Yet, as most religious and ethical systems teach us, the privileging and prioritization of our needs, etc. in this way is not justified. After all, the fact that our beliefs, goals, values, and ideals are our own does not make them more likely to be true, appropriate, or worthy of pursuit. Nor does the fact that we experience our own needs and desires more strongly mean that they actually matter more.

As Mark Johnston wrote:

> The truly ethical life is a life in which you encounter yourself as one person among others, all equally real. This means that the legitimate interests of others, insofar as you can anticipate them, will figure on a par with your own legitimate interests in your practical reasoning…For you will find yourself to be only one of the others, the one you happen to know so much about, thanks to being him or her.

In other words, living an ethical life requires that we encounter our needs, etc. as they truly are—that is, as only one particular set of needs, etc. (albeit, the ones we happen to know best) within a vast, complex, and interconnected universe of living beings, all with equally real and legitimate needs, etc. of their own.[1]

This is where humility comes in.

⁓⁓

Johnston also wrote:

> There is massive consensus across the major religions, that salvation crucially requires overcoming the centripetal force of self-involvement, in order to orient one's life around reality and the real needs of human beings as such.

In other words, the problem with our natural centeredness is that its centripetal force is a source of both epistemic and ethical distortion—that is, it interferes with our ability to orient ourselves towards reality (so that we can accurately perceive, and engage with, the world as it is—as opposed to how we might think, want, or wish it to be—a world in which we are each only an infinitesimal part of a larger whole), as well as our ability to orient ourselves towards other living beings (so that we can accurately perceive, and engage with, them as they are—as beings with needs, etc. as real and legitimate as our own).

Humility, as I have defined and discussed it elsewhere, is an "epistemically and ethically aligned" state of awareness,

1 By "real and legitimate," I mean several things. First, I mean that they exist, whether we believe they do, or want them to, or not. Second, I mean that they exist *as they are*, not as we would think or want or wish them to be. And third, I mean that from a "god's-eye view"—a view in which the needs, etc. of all living beings are present, there are none that are less significant, less "weighty," less worthwhile and meaningful, than our own. They all matter, and they matter equally, even though we do not necessarily experience them this way.

which means that humility is a state of awareness that corrects for these distortions, a state of awareness in which they are silenced. In other words, through humility, our experience of ourselves in relation to (and in relationship with) other living beings, and with the universe as a whole, is freed from the centripetal force naturally generated by our centered-ness.

As a state of awareness, humility is something we can "come into and go out of" (we can be temporarily or momentarily humble), though it is also something that can stabilize into a sort of "standing" or baseline disposition (or virtue), such that our cognition, affect, and behavior are continuously informed and influenced by it.

To say that humility *orients us towards reality* is to say that it enables us to understand and experience the world around us, and ourselves in it, as it is. For example, it allows us to experience ourselves within the larger context of our existence, generating a clear and accurate sense of ourselves as finite, fragile, and imperfect beings, contingent and relationally constituted—part of a vast, complex, and interconnected universe of living beings. This can be experienced spiritually, as a connection to the Divine or some higher force or power, but it can also be experienced more secularly, through an awareness of one's place in, and connection to, the larger natural world and cosmos.

To say that humility *orients us towards others* is to say that it enables us to understand and experience the vast web of interconnected beings (of which we are a part) as just as morally relevant—as worthy of attention, care, and concern—as ourselves. Importantly, this ethical alignment is experienced as an expansion, not a contraction, of the force and scope of our own needs, desires, interests, beliefs, goals, and values. This is because they become interwoven with the needs, desires, interests, beliefs, goals, and values of others—and, as such, they are no longer experienced as separate, in conflict or in competition, but rather as inextricably and necessarily connected and shared.[2]

In other words, the quieting of the biases naturally generated by our centered-ness results in a feeling of deep connection and fellow-concern. We experience ourselves not simply as less than our natural centered-ness would have us believe, but also as more.

Importantly, this suggests that humility is needed not only to combat the distortions that naturally arise from our centered-ness, but also to develop as ethical beings, expanding our capacity for compassion, courage, honesty, generosity, and other virtues.

To see this, consider: The people we identify as moral exemplars are highly attuned and responsive to the needs, etc. of others. They experience them as being as real and legitimate—as likely to be true or worthwhile—as their own. This means, more specifically, that they are able to perceive and properly evaluate the facts as they present themselves with respect to what they ought (or ought not) do. They are also able to properly weigh the needs, etc. of all relevant others in determining what they ought (or ought not) do. Generally speaking, this allows them to *respond ethically* in a given situation—to do the right thing in the right way at the right time for the right reasons.[3]

Accomplishing all of this requires, at its base, an absence

---

2 Research on moral exemplars all over the world has found that they report flourishing as individuals through their facilitation of, and contributions to, the well-being of others, especially those in need. Indeed, these exemplars experienced their own needs and interests as essentially woven into the needs and interests of those around them, in other words, their communities (see, for example, Colby & Damon, 1992; Monroe, 2004, 2011).

3 Admittedly, this presumes a roughly neo-Aristotelian conception of virtue (e.g., Wright & Snow, 2018).

of the distortions that naturally arise from our centered-ness. In other words, it requires a state of awareness which is free of these distortions, in which they have been silenced, so we are able to experience ourselves, others, and the world we live in as they truly are. This makes humility the starting point in our development of virtue, and living an ethical life.

If humility truly is, as I suspect, the starting point, then it is important to identify and understand the types of circumstances and life experiences that are conducive—even necessary—for its cultivation.

One thing that seems pretty clear is the importance of early life experiences. In particular, the importance of close emotional bonding with one's caregivers (which creates what developmental psychologist Darcia Narvaez calls "limbic resonance," the feeling of deep connection to others that allows for shared emotional experiences), and the development of a healthy sense of individual autonomy that is accompanied and supported by a feeling of belonging—to a family, a peer group, a community. This combination helps to create a healthy orientation towards the self, one less inclined towards a narcissistic defense of self-importance and more open to its capacity for self-transcendence.

Beyond such early experiences, it is important to find opportunities to immerse ourselves in "deep caregiving" communities (such as caring for the dying or disabled). In the encountering of the unalterable and unavoidable vulnerability and suffering of those we care for, these experiences bring us face to face with our own finitude, fragility, and dependency. We must learn what is beyond our capacity to change, repair, or solve—or even fully understand. And in so doing, we become more open to the world and to the other living beings we share it with, able to give ourselves up to simply loving what is in front of us, without trying to change or repair it.

In these situations—and others—we gain what philosopher Iris Murdoch called a "selfless respect for reality." Writing along these lines as well, Johnston states:

> There are large-scale defects in human life that no amount of psychological adjustment or practical success can free us from. These include arbitrary suffering, aging (once it has reached the corrosive stage), our profound ignorance of our condition, the isolation of ordinary self-involvement, the vulnerability of everything we cherish to time and chance, and, finally, to untimely death. ...The redeemed life is a form of life in which we are reconciled to these large-scale defects of ordinary life...the idea [that] even in the face of such things there must be a way to go on, keeping faith in the importance of goodness, and an openness to love.

Perhaps not surprisingly, a number of spiritual practices have also been strongly linked to humility. For example, the practice of Mussar (a Jewish spiritual practice that gives concrete instructions on how to live a meaningful and ethical life) actively cultivates humility by teaching us to occupy our "rightful space"—in other words, mindfully occupying a space (physical, verbal, intellectual, emotional, etc.) that leaves appropriate room for others, while at the same time not shrinking away from that which is ours to occupy. Sometimes learning the boundaries of one's "appropriate space" requires a humbling experience—such as when we are thrown back upon ourselves, shamed for our presumption, or (alternatively) reminded of our responsibility, which we may have shirked, to ourselves and others.[4]

Similarly, meditative practices—such as those practiced by Buddhists and other eastern spiritual traditions—facilitate virtue development (and humility, in particular). The dissolution of the self that occurs during advanced meditative practices— where we experience ourselves, not as substantial entities, but as relationally constituted, and thus linked to the joy and suffering of all living beings—generates a fundamental shift in focus outwards, quieting our centeredness and generating increased patience, humor, and compassion for self and others.

Humility is also often cultivated through experiences of awe and gratitude, experiences where we encounter our smallness—such as when we see the earth as it looks from space or visit the Grand Canyon—or the wondrous majesty and beauty of the natural world and all the living beings we encounter in it.

What all these various paths to humility appear to have in common is a *state of awareness*, whether temporary or stable: an awareness that has shifted out of (even dissolved) our default setting of "centered-ness." With it comes the experience of being fully present in the world, with others and ourselves, as we are. The realization that we are each only a fragment of a wondrous whole; that we are each part of an imperfect world—one that we did not make or choose—composed of undefeatable difficulties and insurmountable odds. Only together, can we see the whole—an organic preciousness for which we cannot help but experience love and gratitude. For the beauty of our imperfection, for the grace bestowed upon us by of our suffering, and for the indescribably joyful challenge of being alive.

---

4 An excellent discussion of the practice can be found in *Everyday Holiness* by Alan Morinis.

ZABEULAH'S LESSON

Ruth Nicole Brown

Aunt Dottie's house burst with butterflies. Everywhere you turned there were swallowtails on doilies, Painted Ladies painted on refrigerator magnets, Monarchs grouped in migratory scenes, and Angle Wings stitched on pillows.

The outside not to be outdone by the inside, Aunt Dottie landscaped her yard with colorful mixed-media artistic excess to feature her favorite technique—planting silk flowers among annuals and perennials. Plastic and surely living insects added more color and some movement. Tire pots were painted white to match the painted white tree trunks. The grass was always cut short and edged to perfection.

A small framed two-bedroom house, Aunt Dottie's exceptionally beautified sanctuary was home to many: a butterfly garden. More people than I would ever meet in an Ann Arbor month stopped by to visit daily, announced and unannounced. I believe they stopped by for the same reason I did. Aunt Dottie knew how to love you back, so much so, you were prompted to reflect to ask: if it is blooming time, how might I open up to the necessary beauty needed in the now to fly?

"Ruthie," she called me, "Is it alright if we have McDonald's pancakes in the morning?" Store-bought pancakes served as invitation for me to extend some grace to Aunt Dottie's aging body. She needed to conserve energy in the morning for the day's festivities, which would range from backyard fish fries, all-day church service, and Deacon Street block parties that ran late into the night. We watched *Wheel of Fortune*. We listened to church on the radio. We held long conversations. I listened to my Uncle Jack tell stories about old Detroit and Kresge's factory. Aunt Dottie showed me photographs and shared family memories. In her speech, I searched for and found how she moved, and that's the way I sing, like grace is a fluttering living thing.

Sarah Grace is the name given to me by We Levitate, the band I am in, which makes music from our collective practice. We Levitate calls me "Sarah" because I have four children, which seems of biblical proportion in relation to my career as a professor. Academic culture teaches work-life balance as one of each, not four of anything. "Grace" is the characteristic those in the band most often name when others want to know who I really am in the classroom outside of my performance with the band and Lil' Kim-inspired "Crush On You" blue wig.

Formally trained musicians want to know what instrument I play in the band. But besides our own creative props—which might be a whistle for me, a white dress on Porshé, Jessica's black leggings, and Blair's DJ equipment—I don't play an instrument in a traditional sense. I definitely do not sing on key or with perfect pitch. The sound is a conglomeration of funk, soul, rhythm and blues, gospel, hip hop, and house, and sometimes I sing, speak, and rap. More than anything, I think, we make music that sounds like the gifts we've each been given.

At one of our We Levitate concerts; the dancing went on longer than the flyer stated and we insisted on paying the tax for extended space rental. A homegirl (who has never met Aunt Dottie) and I were driving home, listening to our music on a CD because we just could not get enough. Hungry from the dancehall, she reached in her purse and found some Flamin' Hot Cheetos. After popping the bag open, she extended them in my direction, offering me first dibs. "You, before me," she said. This password, handed down from generation to generation, I recognize immediately. A butterfly overhead.

Zabeulah Carey Wade, who my family called Aunt Dottie, was one of my Grandma Ruth's older sisters. As a girl, I visited Aunt Dottie and Uncle Jack's for family reunions. I relearned the meaning of "neighbor" and was intimately introduced to chosen family. Family photos were intentionally placed and hung throughout the house teeming with keepers of Kentucky and Tennessee traditions. I did not recognize them all but I knew that to them, I belonged.

The more Aunt Dottie gave the more she had to give. It was a negation of self that depended on a complete understanding of generosity divine as trees, gendered feminine outside of patriarchal norms, God-given, disabled, and Black. Carey girls kept house with exacting science and decadent artistry. Each one stretched in a different direction; they kept a profound sweetness in their arsenal and taught new generations of Carey girls their no-nonsense ideas about living through family rituals of gathering on occasions of celebration, mourning, and reunion.

Aunt Dottie made power out of delicate tenderness, speculative impairments, and feelings of deservedness too often denied Black women and girls. Ordinary and extraordinary, she formulated humility from generosity so it could not be reduced to something like low esteem. Something always grows from the conditions of this world. Aunt Dottie's generosity was sourced from a life-affirming humility that, among many things, works as antidote to misunderstanding.

Gossiped about for loving too much, Aunt Dottie was born with her heart on the right side of her chest cavity. That was the first explanation I heard of why she gave differently— as if directed by an astral force, and it didn't seem untrue enough to question. In Pembroke, Kentucky, where she was born with a wrong-sided heart that exuded a correcting love, her exceptionalism was felt and lived through touch. You had no idea when you changed and transformed in her presence, you just knew that it happened. That is all and everything to how her humility means and teaches. The very best given is not to be owned, but added to, and then given away as good weather for flight.

Aunt Dottie and Uncle Jack moved to Detroit for the same reasons as did many others in the 40s—factory work promising economic stability. They brought with them a vibrant sense of the social and profound faith. I do not know what, beyond youthful naiveté, pride, and stress, kept me away from visiting Aunt Dottie and Uncle Jack when I was living and studying in Ann Arbor. I didn't go see Aunt Dottie as my mother encouraged until my third year of graduate school. It had been a while. I was no longer a girl. I had exams. I was trying to be grown.

I saw them enact an economics I did not learn in the course books, yet felt in a real way in heavy pockets. After the three of us held hands in prayer, Aunt Dottie would say, "I know Daddy gave you gas money already, but we can do better than that!" and she would give me a wad of cash. To which Uncle Jack, would say, "Oh Ruthie! We so enjoyed you this weekend," hugging me and handing me some more change. While loading the car, Aunt Dottie would call me back inside of the house and say, "Me and Daddy thought we could do better than we did, so take this and get home safely." I wondered where the money came from—the three of us in the kitchen was a Rubik's cube. This was not a small thing. Even in the grand gesturing of this "you before me" ritual, it was unassuming. They were trusting this Carey namesake to not be distracted by money but available to the lesson of their outgiving ritual.

In the band, I sing so clear in my roundabout way: the social delight as stronghold. I wander the stage motivated by pleasure, coupled with a deep satisfaction that feels like the music hums all over the place. I am giving myself a chance to profess with little expectation of return; there may be no applause. The obvious question—"What is she doing?"—is a question that is Black. In search of how she made this something to be taken in that also fills up is also Blackness. After We Levitate performs and levitation is shared, everyone is freer. That energy transforms me every time.

Selflessness can be distorted, exploited, or denied but, I think about what it means to keep a humble home. Aunt Dottie preserved recipes for vanilla cake with chocolate sauce spooned over top, teacakes, and rolls learned in her girlhood, so that they are now a cherished memory in my own. I too have committed to the rise of baked goods and the raising up of people with the stir and stillness collective work requires. Slow and steady the lyrics come to me through a network of relationships with and among those similarly eager for the taste of fulfilling change. My recipe for nuance includes humility in the way that I learned from Aunt Dottie.

My contribution to the band is to follow the ways of butterflies; reveling in the beauty of smallness and abiding things so delicate they might just break, if not respected and acknowledged—sentiments requiring sensitivity, an aesthetic preference for the habits and ways personnel management might suggest be thrown away, and a politics of delight. Such music I learned as Aunt Dottie's niece was wholly restorative. Even unto herself, a song.

For me, We Levitate's studio practice, where we create and record music, is such a vulnerable ritual because I am not formally trained yet I get to announce all the ways that I am, in the presence of those who see me doing and know that I have never lied to them. In my verses, I hear myself making the block beautiful and uncontained. We extend the moment by promising another.

Zabeulah's lesson is a dotted butterfly that scientists often refer to as *Polygonia interrogationis*. During periods of intense questioning, Zabeulah's lesson will appear so you do not forget humility in the practice. The presence of this butterfly is a message for cultural workers to rename that which you need so that it cannot be weaponized against your dreams and collective impact. Each dot is an instance of us being for each other, and a "you before me" logic whereby humility and giving mean something beautiful when expressed between and among Black women and Black girls. When Zabeulah's lesson lands nearby, it asks you to remember that not everything can be professionalized or commodified.

Zabeulah's lesson sounds like this: Use whatever is most feared to reflect and inform who we say we are as recipe for the rise. The heat is hot and you'll have to be flexible. Skilled in waiting, letting go, and holding on, we can, through the dip and toss, motivate each other. A different version of Sun Ra Arkestra, all of us as Black brown dark matter, popsicle melting, just keep playing. When Black girls go first we are going together. So, give it up. That is a hard and fixed direction in the form of "I can't make it," "I didn't like it," and "Maybe, next time," and "What in the world?!". Extend with patience some call grace. Stand supported by artifice and artifact. The sound of a healthy selflessness or what I understand to be a queer practice of self-abnegation, resists the kind of self-regard on which status quo algorithms of humility depend. You have to listen for it always and especially when hungry.

Notice Zabeulah's lesson. Feel the delight of us being for each other and inspiring both rest and movement. The dotted markings of care are evident, complete incoherent ciphers of other ways, including yours. To be trusted.

in order to
learn and unlearn

LOVING KNOWLEDGE TOGETHER: SOCRATIC HUMILITY

Agnes Callard

P hilosophers aren't the only ones who love wisdom. Everyone, philosopher or not, loves *her own* wisdom: the wisdom she has or takes herself to have. What distinguishes the philosopher is loving the wisdom she *doesn't* have. Philosophy is, therefore, a form of humility: being aware that you lack what is of supreme importance. There may be no human being who exemplified this form of humility more perfectly than Socrates. It is no coincidence therefore, that he is considered the first philosopher within the Western canon.

Socrates did not write philosophy—he simply went around talking to people. But these conversations were so transformative that the second Western philosopher, Plato, devoted his life to writing dialogues that represent Socrates in conversation. These dialogues are not transcripts of actual conversations, but they are nonetheless clearly intended to reflect not only Socrates' ideas but his personality. Plato wanted the world to remember Socrates. Generations after Socrates' death, warring philosophical schools such as the Stoics and the Skeptics each appropriated Socrates as figurehead. Though they disagreed on just about every point of doctrine, they were clear that in order to count themselves as philosophers they had to somehow be working in the tradition of Socrates.

47

What is it about Socrates that made him into a symbol for the whole institution of philosophy? Consider the fact that, when the oracle at Delphi proclaims Socrates wisest of men, he tries to prove it wrong:

> I went to one of those reputed wise, thinking that there, if anywhere, I could refute the oracle and say to it: "This man is wiser than I, but you said I was." Then, when I examined this man—there is no need for me to tell you his name, he was one of our public men—my experience was something like this: I thought that he appeared wise to many people and especially to himself, but he was not. I then tried to show him that he thought himself wise, but that he was not. As a result he came to dislike me, and so did many of the bystanders. So I withdrew and thought to myself: "I am wiser than this man; it is likely that neither of us knows anything worthwhile, but he thinks he knows something when he does not, whereas when I do not know, neither do I think I know; so I am likely to be wiser than he to this small extent, that I do not think I know what I do not know.[5]

If Socrates' trademark *claim* is this protestation of ignorance, his trademark *activity* is the one also described in this passage: refuting the views of others. These are the conversations we find in Plato's texts. How are the claim and the activity related? Socrates denies that his motivations are altruistic: he says he is not a teacher,[6] and insists that he is himself the primary beneficiary of the conversations he initiates.[7] This adds to the mystery: what is Socrates getting out of showing people that they don't know what they take themselves to know? What's his angle?

5 Plato, *Apology* 21cd
6 Plato, *Apology* 33a
7 Plato, *Charmides* 166d

Over and over again, Socrates approaches people who are remarkable for their lack of humility—which is to say, for the fact that they feel confident in their own knowledge of what is just, or pious, or brave, or moderate. You might have supposed that Socrates, whose claim to fame is his awareness of his own ignorance, would treat these self-proclaimed "wise men" (Sophists) with contempt, hostility or indifference. But he doesn't. The most remarkable feature of Socrates' approach is his punctilious politeness and sincere enthusiasm. The conversation usually begins with Socrates asking his interlocutor, "Since you think you know, can you tell me, what *is* courage (or wisdom or piety or justice …)?" Over and over again, it turns out that they think they can answer, but they can't. Socrates' hope springs eternal: even as he walks toward the courtroom to be tried (and eventually put to death) for his philosophical activity, he is delighted to encounter the self-important priest Euthyphro, who will, surely, be able to say what piety is. (Spoiler: he's not.)

Socrates seemed to think that the people around him could help him acquire the knowledge he so desperately wanted—even though they were handicapped by the illusion that they already knew it. Indeed, I believe that their ill-grounded confidence was precisely what drew Socrates to them. If you think you know something, you will be ready to speak on the topic in question. You will hold forth, spout theories, make claims … and all this, under Socrates' relentless questioning, is the way to actually acquire the knowledge you had deluded yourself into thinking you already had.

Let me sketch a little dialogue you might have with Socrates.

Socrates: What is courage?

You: Courage is being willing to take big risks without knowing how it's going to work out.

Socrates: Such as risking your life?

You: Yes.

Socrates: Is courage good?

You: Yes.

Socrates: Do you want it for yourself and your children?

You: Yes.

Socrates: Do you want your children to go around risking their lives?

You: No. Maybe I should've said that courage is taking prudent risks, where you know what you are doing.

Socrates: Like an expert investor who knows how to risk money to make lots more?

You: No, that isn't courageous ...

At this point, your pathways are blocked. You cannot say courage is ignorant risk-taking, and you can't say courage is prudent-risk taking. You do not have a way forward. You are in what Socrates' interlocutors called "aporia," a state of confusion in which there is nowhere for you to go.

Suppose the conversation goes no further than this—suppose, as is typical for Socrates' interlocutors, that you storm off in a huff at this point. Where does that leave you, and where does that leave Socrates? Let's start with you. You might be in a worse mood than you were when you encountered Socrates, but he hasn't harmed you. In fact, you are better off than you were: you've learned that courage isn't as easy to define as you initially thought it was. Being improved isn't always pleasant. Second, Socrates has learned something. Courage seems to involve something like endurance or holding fast, but it cannot straightforwardly be identified with such a state—not even when we add some other ingredients, such as wisdom. Before this conversation, Socrates didn't know what courage was. Now his ignorance can take a more specific shape: he doesn't know what the connection between courage and endurance is. He still knows that he doesn't know what courage is, but his knowledge of his own ignorance has been improved, made more precise.

It's one thing to say, "I don't know anything." That thought comes cheap. One can wonder, "Who really and truly knows anything?" in a way that is dismissive, uninquisitive, detached. It can be a way of saying, "Knowledge is unattainable, so why even try?" Socratic humility is more expensive and more committal than that. He sought to map the terrain of his ignorance, to plot its mountains and its rivers, to learn to navigate it. That, I think, is why he speaks of *knowledge* of his own ignorance. But this is a paradoxical project. It's one thing to be missing your wallet—that seems like something you can know. But suppose you're missing not only your wallet, but also the knowledge that you ever had a wallet, and the understanding of what a wallet is. Can you know that you don't know all that? Can you map in total darkness?

Socrates' answer was no. Or at least: you can't do it alone. The right response to noticing one's own ignorance is to try to escape it by acquiring someone else's knowledge. But the only way to do that is to explain to them why you aren't yet able to accept this or that claim of theirs as knowledge—and that is what mapping one's ignorance amounts to. It's when he refutes others' claims to knowledge that Socrates' own ignorance takes shape, for him, as something he can know. What appears as a sea of darkness when approached introspectively turns out to be navigable when brought into contact with the knowledge-claims of another.

Socrates was an unusual person. Consider his response to the oracle. Most people who are proclaimed wise by a trusted authority don't have the impulse to disprove that authority. Instead, they bask in the glory of the assessment of themselves that they have spent their whole lives longing to hear. Most people steer conversations into areas where they have expertise; they struggle to admit error; they have a background confidence that they have a firm grip on the basics. They are happy to think of other people—people who have different political or religious views, or got a different kind of education, or live in a different part of the world—as ignorant and clueless. They are eager to claim the status of knowledge for everything they themselves think.

But Socrates did not take this difference as grounds to despise or dismiss this group, aka Most People (hoi polloi). He saw, instead, that he and Most People were a match made in heaven. Most People put forward claims, and Socrates refutes them. Most People see the need to possess truths. Socrates saw the danger of acquiring falsehoods. Most People feel full of rich insights and brilliant thoughts. Socrates saw himself as bereft of all of that. Without the help of Most People, Socrates wouldn't have anything to think about. Socrates' neediness did not escape Socrates' own notice. In the *Theaetetus*, he describes himself as a kind of midwife—barren of knowledge himself, but engaged in "delivering" the wisdom-babies of Most People.

Socrates saw the pursuit of knowledge as a collaborative project involving two very different roles. There's you or I or some other representative of Most People, who comes forward and makes a bold claim. Then there's Socrates, or one of his contemporary descendants, who questions and interrogates and distinguishes and calls for clarification. This is something we're still doing—as philosophers, as scientists, as interviewers, on Twitter and Facebook and in many casual personal conversations. We're constantly probing one another, asking, "How can you say that, given XYZ?" We're still trying to understand one another by way of objection, clarification, and the simple fact of inability to take what was said as knowledge. It comes so naturally to us to organize ourselves into the knower/objector pairing that we don't even notice we are living in the world that Socrates made. The scope of his influence is remarkable. But equally remarkable is the means by which it was achieved: he did so much by knowing, writing, and accomplishing—*nothing at all.*

Plato depicts Socrates' final moments in the *Phaedo.* Before he fulfills his death sentence by drinking the hemlock, he offers up a series of arguments about the immortality of the soul. Each argument attempts to improve upon the previous one's failure to show the people around him that his death is not something to be mourned. Despite the brilliance, refinement, and detail of argumentation, he does not convince his interlocutors. From much experience teaching and reading the dialogue, I can say that he does not convince its readers, either. Arguably, he does not even manage to convince himself. He died as he lived, ignorant and inquiring.

EDUCATION IS A SPACE TO CHANGE YOUR MIND

Troy Jollimore

I am, by profession, a professor of philosophy. One of the texts I teach most often in my classes, and with the greatest degree of pleasure, is Plato's *Apology*. The *Apology* consists, essentially, of the speech Socrates made in his own defense at his trial in ancient Athens—the trial that famously ended with his conviction and execution. As part of his address to the Athenian jury, Socrates tells a story about the oracle at Delphi. According to this story within a story, an acquaintance of Socrates asked the oracle who the wisest man in Athens was, and was met with the response that no man was wiser than Socrates. Socrates, by his own account, could not believe this was so. He went about questioning those residents of Athens whom he took to be wiser than himself. What he found, though, after many conversations, was that these reputedly wise persons were not as wise as they believed.

"My experience was something like this: I thought that he appeared wise to many people and especially to himself, but he was not…. So I withdrew and thought to myself: 'I am wiser than this man; it is likely that neither of us knows anything worthwhile, but he thinks he knows something when he does not, whereas when I do not know, neither do I think I know; so I am likely to be wiser than he to this small extent, that I do not think I know what I do not know."

The *Apology* is a compelling and even a fun read, introducing students to two of the most significant thinkers in the Western philosophical tradition, and containing a number of interesting arguments having to do with the nature of courage and of death, what attitude we should take toward death, and other weighty matters. But my main reason for teaching it is something else. Mostly, what I want students to notice about the Socrates of the *Apology* is his humility, and the connection he makes between intellectual humility and wisdom. To fail to realize how little we know, Socrates argues, is to allow ourselves to be content with what we already believe, which we mistakenly but confidently take to be true; and we are unlikely, in such a state, to question ourselves or continue to seek wisdom. In his view, the arrogantly self-assured's failure to be humble is a kind of intellectual complacency. The wise person, by contrast, recognizes the limits of their knowledge, and takes seriously the possibility that they might be mistaken even with respect to those matters about which they feel most confident.

In short, what I want is for my students to take seriously the idea that boundless self-confidence in one's own judgment and opinions might not be as attractive, or as desirable, as it is sometimes made out to be. This is an important thing for philosophy students to keep in mind, and philosophers as well. We often have, after all, a certain tendency to become attached to our opinions and our favored positions, to cleave to them as we would to a lover or a sports team. We have a tendency to stand by our beliefs and commitments, to want to defend them to death, and to be unable to take differing and opposing views and ideas seriously, to give them a fair hearing.

That's why, when I talk to my philosophy students about these matters, I like to tell them about Philippa Foot. Foot was one of my favorite twentieth-century philosophers, in part because she was a brilliant philosopher, but for another reason as well. One of her best known and most influential papers was titled "Morality as a System of Hypothetical Imperatives." It was published in the early 1970s. In the 1990s, Foot allowed it to be republished in an anthology only on the condition that she was allowed to add a postscript, which she titled "Recantation 1994."

"The idea that morality is a system of hypothetical imperatives," she begins, "is so alien to my present views that I no longer want to reprint this paper without explaining that I have long thought the positive part of it misconceived." She goes on to explain how, when she wrote that paper, she was under the sway of certain faulty philosophical presuppositions that prevented her from seeing things that, she writes, "anyone innocent of philosophy" would have seen. Most strikingly of all, she ends her "recantation" by directing her readers to a paper by Gavin Lawrence which, she acknowledges, constitutes "an excellent criticism" of her earlier article.

Not only was Foot an excellent philosopher, she was also humble, in a manner and to a degree that I find inspiring, even moving. Indeed, she was such an excellent philosopher, in part, because she was humble. It was this humility—this willingness to take seriously the possibility that her most firmly held beliefs might be wrong, and her open-mindedness toward the thoughts of others who were critical of those beliefs—that allowed her to change her views over time, to improve her thinking, to get closer to the truth. It was to the truth, rather than to her own positions or reputation, that she was genuinely committed.

I always have some students who are surprised by Foot's behavior. Some of them are overtly critical of it. They think that Foot should have stood by her position, that she was being inconsistent, or weak, in changing her mind. Two or three of them, over the years, have accused her of a lack of integrity, as if having integrity required us to close our eyes and ears to available evidence, as if it required us, once we had reached a certain fixed point of firm belief, to stop thinking. One of them called her a "flip-flopper," an accusation frequently leveled against political candidates in this country, where "standing for something," even when that something goes against the available evidence, is all too frequently seen as a virtue, while changing one's mind and admitting that one was wrong—something that any thoughtful or, for that matter, minimally rational person has to do from time to time—is likely to be portrayed by one's opponents as a sign of emptiness and weakness.

In having students consider these ideas, I often feel a certain resistance. Indeed, it frequently seems that I am swimming against powerful currents. Many of my students' previous teachers, not to mention their parents, role models, and peers, have given them the idea that a boundless self-confidence in their own judgment and opinions is a very good thing indeed: an attitude they need to develop in order to be happy and successful, and an attitude that, as Americans, they are both entitled and obliged to hold. Every semester I teach a section or two of Health Ethics, and I am inevitably faced with a handful of students—sometimes just a couple, sometimes several—who are perplexed, bewildered, and to some degree outraged by the idea that a paper in which they expressed their sincere opinions on euthanasia, genetic enhancement, the distribution of health care resources, or what have you, might receive less than a perfect grade. "But this is morality," I was recently told by one such student, who was mystified that he had received a C on his paper rather than the A he believed he deserved for describing (with, it must be said, very little by way of argument or support) his own thoughts on these matters. "It's all just opinion. There are no wrong answers here."

"Let me ask you this," I said to him. "If it really were the case that there were no right or wrong answers in this area, no better or worse answers, no stronger or weaker arguments or reasons for believing one thing as opposed to another, then how could it make sense for people to devote their entire careers to studying these things? Why would people put so much time and energy into conducting studies and publishing books trying to determine what works better and what doesn't, or what we should do and what we shouldn't do? Does that really make sense?"

Does it matter, though, whether this makes sense? After all, for this student, as for many students today, it is precisely the idea of expertise—in this area, and perhaps anywhere—that does not make sense. What some can't accept is the idea that there are aspects of reality so complicated that they cannot be quickly and intuitively mastered by anyone with good instincts and a little bit of gumption. Things are worse, of course, in moral philosophy, where many young people have been taught from the very start that all morality is relative, just a matter of opinion, with no right or wrong answers to be had. What I suspect many of my students think—and I have had at least a couple say it to my face—is that the whole business of moral philosophy, like so many expert-employing industries, is pure sham, a made-up endeavor through and through, something we have created out of thin air to give ourselves jobs and to command respect, to cement a place in society without having to do any constructive or useful work. But even where they are prepared to acknowledge that right and wrong answers might exist, the idea that such answers are hard to find—that it might require years of study and intellectual preparation—is hard for these students to accept. Indeed, they find it deeply objectionable; it flies in the face of their democratic instincts. As Isaac Asimov once wrote, for many Americans, the meaning of "democracy" pretty much boils down to the idea that "my ignorance is just as good as your knowledge."

In asserting the equivalence of their ignorance to the well-informed positions of others, these students are simply expressing attitudes they have absorbed from the very air around them, attitudes that are prevalent and pervasive in society today. In 2016, during the election campaign, the very successful cartoonist and author Scott Adams—creator of Dilbert—tweeted the following:

> "If experience is necessary for being president, name a political topic I can't master in one hour under the tutelage of top experts."

The sheer hubris of such a remark—the complete and utter lack of humility—is quite astonishing. It is connected to, indeed presupposes, a profound failure to grasp the overwhelming complexity of the world we live in. (One can't help but wonder, incidentally, just what the phrase "top expert" means to someone who thinks that the most complex of subjects, at least in the political realm, can be mastered in an hour.) Having grown up in a social universe in which their successful elders say such things, it is inevitable that many young people today find Socratic humility not only inaccessible but undesirable, and likely unpalatable. They have been assured, from the start, that the world is fundamentally simple, really not very hard to understand. Against that background belief, the idea of developing expertise, of the slow pursuit of knowledge, of intellectual struggle—the idea of higher education itself—is incomprehensible. If you think any topic can be mastered in an hour, and then are told that you need to spend four years to get a university degree, you will naturally assume that most of those four years will consist of wasted time.

In my first year of teaching I heard, from one of my students, a complaint that has often been repeated in the intervening years. Something I was teaching rubbed her the wrong way: it seemed, to her, irrelevant to her concerns. "I'll never use this," she informed me. "This has nothing to do with me." She was indignant, perhaps at the thought that I was wasting her time, and perhaps, more fundamentally, at the very idea that someone might want her to know about something she has no pre-existing interest in. Indignant, perhaps, at the very idea that someone wanted to teach her to be able to think well. The idea that someone might have thought that having a rudimentary knowledge of the history that has brought us to the place we are now, or the ability to access and appreciate the greatest treasures of our culture, might inform and improve her values and decisions—might, indeed, enrich her life—was not only alien to her, it was objectionable.

Can a twenty-year-old, give or take a year or two, know himself so well, and know so much of life, and of the world, to know exactly who he is and what his life will be and how he will bring that about—and that he will never change his mind and decide that in fact, he might want something else—and are thus able to firmly reject what is being offered to him, offered by someone who has quite a bit more experience of life than he does and who believes that what is being offered is, in fact, of immense value? If so, it must be quite a dizzying experience. I have come, more and more, over the course of my teaching career, to think that my primary goal is to cure that dizziness, to undermine that wild confidence, to simply make it go away.

I would not want to give the impression that all of my students are this self-assured. Some of them do, indeed, seem to arrive at university with some comprehension of the vastness and complexity of the universe and the modesty of the human capacity for knowledge in the face of that vastness. My impression, though, is that students who have somehow managed to attain this have for the most part done so by going against, not with, the grain of the society in which they have been enculturated. Depending on the details of their university careers—depending on what they end up studying, what particular classes they find themselves in, and who they happen to encounter along the way—the education they receive there might, and might not, help them maintain their grasp on this precious knowledge. That, like so many things in higher education these days, will be in large part a matter of chance.

These are hard days for higher education. Anyone will tell you that. They are also, as we all know, hard days for our society and culture. People have a hard time listening to each other. They find it hard to treat people with whom they disagree with respect, or to take diverging views seriously. They have so much self-confidence in their own opinions that they are unable to be self-critical, and the existence of people who hold different opinions strikes them as disturbing, as a kind of affront. I am generalizing, of course; not everyone in our country suffers from these maladies. But a great many contemporary Americans seem to see themselves as possessing an astoundingly deep and impressive grasp of highly complex matters, including, often, matters they have spent little if any time studying or learning about. And they tend to rate their own grasp of complex matters much more highly than they regard the understandings of those around them—including, frequently, people who have spent a good deal of time studying the matters in question.

In a 2017 *New Yorker* article titled "Why Facts Don't Change Our Minds," Elizabeth Kolbert describes a 2014 survey, conducted shortly after the Russian annexation of Crimea, in which respondents were asked how they thought the US should react, and also whether they could identify Ukraine on a map. The farther off base they were about the geography, the more likely they were to favor military intervention. (Respondents were so unsure of Ukraine's location that the median guess was wrong by 1,800 miles, roughly the distance from Kiev to Madrid.)

The crucial sentence is of course the second one: knowing less about the situation—the very basic facts about the situation, like where in the world it is that we are talking about—makes people more likely to have strong opinions, or at least, a certain very dangerous sort of strong opinion, about what ought to be done. This result might perhaps be paired with a 2015 poll in which more than thirty percent of Republican primary voters and nearly twenty percent of Democratic primary voters said they supported bombing Agrabah. Agrabah, let's be clear, is not a real place. It is the name of the fictional country in the Disney animated film *Aladdin*.

But the right to one's opinion about whether or not military intervention in the Ukraine or Agrabah is justified—

whether or not one knows where the Ukraine or Agrabah are, or whether they really exist or not—is held by many to be sacrosanct; it is the right to hold the belief that matters to them, not the content of the belief. Indeed, the idea that everyone has the right to their own opinion—which is surely true in some important sense—has somehow come to be widely understood as the view that all opinions are equally good. And in many contexts, this has given rise not to an appreciation of diverse viewpoints, but to its opposite: an angry intolerance of any views that conflict with one's own, and a habit of dismissing such views without giving them much, if any, consideration.

This seems self-contradictory. After all, if everyone's opinions are equally good, then other people's opinions are no worse than yours, and it is absurd to disparage them. But from a different angle, this viewpoint makes perfect sense. After all, if all opinions are equally good, then (1) there is nothing wrong with your opinion, whatever it might be, and (2) the opinion that those who disagree with you are idiots is also as good as any other opinion. And if, in general, all opinions are equally good, then the opinions you already have are as good as any set of opinions can be. They could not be better, and there is no possibility for improvement. So working to improve one's opinions and beliefs (let alone spending four years in college to do so) will strike one, necessarily, as a waste of time. If we believe that all opinions are equally good— a belief that stands in radical opposition to Socrates' view, that we should recognize how little we know and how easily we can be wrong—the idea of correcting errors and improving one's beliefs simply makes no sense whatsoever. Indeed, the very idea of listening to others, of paying serious attention to them, may well come to seem a pointless exercise, a waste of time.

Socrates' advantage over his fellow Athenians was his knowledge of his own intellectual limits. Along with this, and inseparable from it, he had—for his time, and certainly relative to those around him—an admirable sense of perspective, a sense of what an overwhelming and mysterious place the world is, of the way that the world dwarfs the human capacity for understanding. If the gods spoke directly to us, he tells us in the *Apology*, they would probably say that "human wisdom is worth little or nothing" and that "That man among you, mortals, is wisest who, like Socrates, understands that his wisdom is worthless."

I am not sure that Socrates truly believed that his wisdom was worthless; he quite clearly thought, at any rate, that the pursuit of wisdom was the most worthwhile of human activities. The thing about the pursuit of wisdom, though, is that it requires humility; it requires that you believe that you are not already wise, or at least that you could become wiser. It requires that you recognize that knowing where Agrabah is, and whether it exists, ought to be regarded as a necessary prerequisite for having a strong opinion about what should be done about it. It requires that we work toward developing a sense of the world as a vast and complex place that we can, and ought to, continue to learn about for the rest of our lives without ever coming to master. And it requires us, on a daily basis, to commit ourselves to the difficult work of taking our fellow human beings seriously; the perpetual task of listening, with a fair mind and open ears, to people whose backgrounds, ideas, and opinions may be uncomfortably different from our own.

TRUMP, ARROGANCE, AND AMERICAN DEMOCRACY

Charles M. Blow

'll start by acknowledging that presidents lie. Politicians lie, people lie. But there is no equivalent to the person who served as our forty-fifth president. The truth is constantly shifting beneath this man's feet like sand. He has no regard for the firmness of fact. To him, truth is pliant.

Indeed PolitiFact named Trump's collective campaign misstatements their 2015 lie of the year. They wrote, "It's the trope on Trump: He's authentic, a straight-talker, less scripted than traditional politicians. That's because Donald Trump doesn't let facts slow him down. Bending the truth or being unhampered by accuracy is a strategy he has followed for years." The site quoted from Trump's book *The Art of the Deal* in which Trump says [through a ghostwriter, because of course he didn't write that book], "People want to believe that something is the biggest and the greatest and the most spectacular. I call it truthful hyperbole … [euphemism for lying] It's an innocent form of exaggeration—and a very effective form of promotion." But in politics that's called propaganda. And it is not so innocent.

In fact, Tony Schwartz, the ghostwriter for that book, told Jane Mayer of *The New Yorker* in July 2016 that Trump lies strategically. " 'He had a complete lack of conscience about it.' Since most people are 'constrained by the truth,' Trump's indifference to it 'gave him a strange advantage.' " But I'm going to argue that it's not that strange at all, but intentional and tactical. When introducing a series about the scale and depth of Trump's lies, *New Yorker* magazine's editor David Remnick put it this way, "Donald Trump ... does not so much struggle with truth as strangle it altogether. He lies to avoid. He lies to inflame. He lies to promote and to preen. Sometimes he seems to lie just for the hell of it. He traffics in conspiracy theories that he cannot possibly believe and in grotesque promises that he cannot possibly fulfill. When found out, he changes the subject—or lies larger."

This gets into the three ways in which Trump lies. One, is the lying larger. It is the incredible psychological trick that Adolf Hitler called the big lie. Everybody tells small lies so we are incredibly attuned at catching them.

Did you eat my leftover Chinese food in the refrigerator?
No, I didn't eat it.
You're the only person here. You ate it.

But if you tell a big lie, the brain says, "I cannot believe that somebody would lie that big." So it searches for truth in the lie. Even when it cannot find truth in the lie, it vests faith in part of the lie because it refuses to believe that somebody would lie that big.

The second way Trump lies is by preponderance: sheer volume. When PolitiFact did their analysis of Trump's campaign statements, they found that only four percent were absolutely true. *The Washington Post* went through his public statements at the 466-day mark of his presidency and found that he was lying, on average, 6.5 lies a day. Psychologists describe this as "cognitive load." The brain becomes overloaded and can't work fast enough to figure out what part of the statement is a lie, and why it is a lie. It becomes exhausted and gives up. And the moment that it gives up, some of the lies seep in and become believable.

The third way, is pretending that he is not the producer of the lies, but just the projector of those lies. You've probably heard some of these phrases: "People are saying …," "People told me … ," " "Someone told me…," "People have written…," "I heard…" These are shields that prevent him from ever being blamed for the lies in which he traffics.

But not only does he speak out of a lack of respect for the truth and for honesty, he also speaks out of a lack of knowledge about scholarship and history.

Forget for a moment that the ghostwriter said, "I seriously doubt that Trump has ever read a book straight through in his adult life." This is believable. Have you ever heard him make a literary reference? Forget for a moment that he gathered one of the least educated cabinets in recent memory. Focus instead on the anti-intellectual and historical things that he has said himself. He claims to have invented worn idioms. "Fake news" is his apparently. He "primed the pump." He said he invented that. Though that term was invented in the 1800s by a liberal economist. Trump went on a tear about the Civil War: "People don't ask that question, but why was there a Civil War?"

You could fill a stadium with books about the Civil War. People have asked about it since there was a Civil War. Trump says that Andrew Jackson was a tough guy. He could've made a deal that prevented the Civil War. Andrew Jackson? Responsible for Trail of Tears, Andrew Jackson? Slave owning Andrew Jackson? Andrew Jackson was not winding down his use of slaves, but was increasing his ownership until he died. He had ten times more slaves when he died than when he was a young man. What deal would he have made? The Civil

War has slavery at its base. You can make arguments about whether or not people fought about the immortality of slavery, or whether they fought about the southern economy being built on slavery, or whether they fought about states' rights to determine whether they would have slavery or not, but slavery is at the base of all of those questions. And so what is the deal Jackson would have made? What is the halfway point between free and slave? I don't know of a semi-slavery.

The lie that still stays with me is Trump seeming to not know who Frederick Douglass was and, therefore, believing that he may still be alive. Frederick Douglass, who died in 1895, "is an example of somebody who's done an amazing job." Fredrick Douglass is a monumental American figure. Not just a Black figure. He's an American figure. If social media existed when Frederick Douglass was alive, he'd have been the king of it. He learned how to navigate the media of his time. He owned two newspapers in his life. He was an incredibly sought-after and brilliant orator. He wrote an amazing autobiography. He is the most photographed American of the 1900s. Period. Black, white, male, female, politician, star of stage, no one. Everybody knows who Frederick Douglass was, except our current President.

But more importantly, Trump could learn so much from the relationship that Frederick Douglass had with Abraham Lincoln.

Douglass was a vicious critic of Abraham Lincoln. Lincoln does not start off as the most egalitarian fellow. He was very much an accommodationist. When he starts his political life, he was not in any way interested in emancipation of the slaves. In fact, in his first inauguration address, he talks about the responsibility to return runaway slaves who get to free states back to their master slave owners in the slave states. This incenses Frederick Douglass, who writes, among other things, a blistering essay in which he calls Lincoln an excellent slave hound. For Frederick Douglass, this is personal. Frederick Douglass is a runaway. He continues to blast and blast and blast and blast Lincoln. And one of Fredrick Douglass' hobbyhorses was his advocacy for Black people to be able to join the military and to fight.

Someone invites Douglass to D.C. to talk about this military point and Lincoln grants him an audience in the White House. Now think about that. He's a fierce critic. He's writing the most horrible things that he can possibly write about you. You have said in your inaugural address you should return free, runaway slaves back to the south, to the states, and to their owners. He's a runaway slave who is writing horrible things about you and, yet, you invite your fiercest critic into the White House and you listen. Douglass wasn't particularly blown away by what Lincoln said but, he recounted, that at least he listened and treated me with respect.

Over the years, they become very close friends and I believe Douglass had an incredible impact on Lincoln's thinking about the institution of slavery. At one point, Lincoln calls Douglass "the most meritorious man in the United States." At Lincoln's second inauguration, Douglass chooses to attend the after-party, which was then open to the public. But the country's still not that free. Douglass shows up and the cops grab his arms—what is this Black man doing at this after party? A friend rushes in to let Lincoln know about the ruckus and, within a minute, Douglass is invited into the East Room where Lincoln booms across the room, "Here comes my friend Douglass."

Think about the amount of growth involved in that relationship and what it can mean for you to just be open enough, humble enough, to listen to someone who you disagree with? To admit that you might have been wrong, and to be brave enough to change your mind.

A President who read books might know this. But Trump was a president who wanted absolute control over the flow of information to dictate his own version of fact, rather than to live by the reality of established fact.

as an alternative to hierarchy

RECONSTRUCTING HUMILITY: FROM OBEDIENCE TO RESPECT

Aaron Ahuvia and Jeremy Wood

Judging from the frequency with which the words "humility," "humble," and "pride" are used in print, the past 200 years have not been kind to these terms. The decrease in usage of the word "pride" even continued throughout the 1960s and 70s despite the attention that the Black Pride, Gay Pride, and other pride movements received at that time. What happened?

The idea of humility has a dark and largely forgotten past that proponents of humility (such as ourselves) should be mindful of. There is a kind of old-school humility that, in the words of St. Thomas Aquinas, consisted of "keeping oneself within one's own bounds, not reaching out to things above one, but submitting to one's superior,"[8] i.e. stay in your place, do as you're told, and for heaven's sake. . . *don't get uppity.* Other major pre-modern thinkers, such as Dante, shared Aquinas' views, and saw the lack of humility (i.e. presence of pride) as not just *a* sin, but *the* sin that underlies all other sins. Since all sins were seen as forms of disobedience to God, and all disobedience stemmed from a lack of humility (an unwillingness to do as you're told), the sin of pride was seen as the prerequisite for all other sins.

8 Summa Contra Gent., bk. IV, ch. lv, tr. Joseph Rickaby.

USE OF **TERMS** IN **PRINT**
1808 - 2008

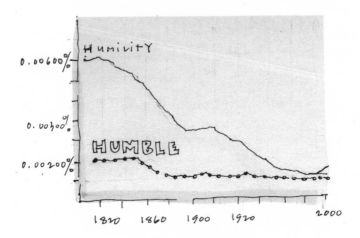

HUMILITY

HUMBLE

0.00600%

0.00300%

0.00200%

1820   1860   1900   1920   2000

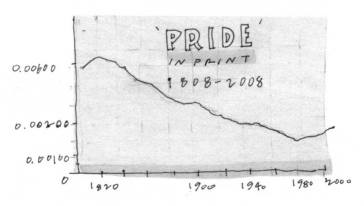

`PRIDE`
IN PRINT
1808 - 2008

0.00600

0.00200

0.00100

0

1820   1900   1940   1980   2000

SOURCE: GOOGLE BOOKS
NGRAM VIEWER

Thus, Saint Augustine wrote, "It was pride that changed angels into devils; it is humility that makes men as angels."

In the 1930s, white southern groups such as the Daughters of the Confederacy erected monuments to their pro-slavery heroes. These monuments mostly depict Confederate leaders. But the monument to Heyward Shepard is an odd exception. Heyward Shepard was a Black man who opposed an effort to free slaves; in fact, he was killed opposing an Abolitionist raid. The Daughters of the Confederacy built a monument to him in 1931, proclaiming that Shepard exemplified "thousands of Negroes who under many temptations throughout subsequent years of war, so conducted themselves that no stain was left upon a record which is the peculiar heritage of the American people, and an everlasting tribute to the best in both races." To the Daughters of the Confederacy, Shepard was a paragon of virtue. And, even if they didn't name it as such, the virtue they had in mind was that traditional, "stay in your place," kind of humility.

From our contemporary perspective, it's easy to be a bit horrified by this older notion of humility. But before we judge too harshly, let's practice a little humility (in the sense of the term we advocate) and try to see things from Aquinas', Dante's, and Augustine's perspective. The world they lived in was far more violent, cruel, and lawless than life in the wealthy West is today. For example, historical evidence suggests that a medieval Englishperson was forty times as likely to be murdered than are English people today.[9] Part of the problem was that the pre-modern police and justice systems couldn't enforce the law effectively. Hence, getting people to follow the rules was a hair's-on-fire level emergency. To this end, religious thinkers ratcheted up the divine retribution sinners would supposedly receive in the afterlife to including gruesome

9 Pinker, Steven (2007), "A History of Violence," *The New Republic*, March 19, https://newrepublic.com/article/77728/history-violence.

torture (yes, we're thinking of those Bruegel paintings too), in the hopes of deterring bad behavior. The idea that humility meant virtuous obedience to authority, in contrast to the sin of prideful disobedience, makes sense in a culture where individual choice was feared as the foundation of a very real epidemic of lawlessness and cruelty.

What are we to make of this older type of humility? Why has it fallen out of favor? Has it really gone, or just receded into the background? And why is a reconstructed notion of humility so badly needed today?

What are we to make of this type of humility? The idea that it was virtuous to "stay in your place" made sense in an earlier society in which everyone was seen as having an unchanging station in the social hierarchy. This was each person's "natural" place, so reaching above your station threw nature out of kilter. For most people, this idea of having a natural place or station within society wasn't just an abstraction. They experienced their assigned place in society as their authentic identity. Hence, as the idea that people should stay in their place fell out of favor, the entire notion of one's authentic identity, i.e. who you *truly* are, underwent a revolution of its own.

We have undergone a vast cultural change since industrialization that sociologists call the shift from an *assigned* to an *achieved identity*. Consider typical people living in medieval Europe. Then, as now, their sense of identity would reflect where they lived, who their friends were, how they earned their daily bread, what their religion was, how they dressed, who they married, how many children they had, etc. But in the past, all these aspects of their identity would have largely been assigned to them. For example, their parents would have picked whom they married, tradition and their social class would have determined their food and clothing, and the number of children they would have had was a biological roll of the dice.

Today, especially in the industrialized West, we have much more choice about where we live, how we will dress, whom we will marry (if anyone), how many children we will have, what our political views will be, what we will read, listen to, and watch, if we will be religious and, if so, what religion we will practice, etc. And choose we do. For example, an astonishing seventy percent of adult Americans identify with a religious denomination[10] that differs from the one they were born into.

Despite this massive cultural change in the West, we have come upon two interesting tidbits of data that suggest that the old "be obedient" conception of humility still operates in some non-Western cultures, and still lurks in the background in the wealthy West. I [meaning Aaron Ahuvia], along with some colleagues, recently completed a study on pride using interview data collected from Americans, Australians, and Indians. One question asked respondents to imagine a scene depicting the positive aspects of pride. US and Australian answers were fairly predictable in the sense that people were happy because they were proud of themselves and their accomplishments. But the answer from one Indian respondent was both surprising and telling in its focus on pride as the ability to make your own choices rather than following social convention or the demands of others:

> The picture depicting pride is of "A house in the woods." People living here would be happy that they have such a thing, and maybe they are a bit far from the city, or *they live in a place where they are alone*. So just they live in a wood house. So, it's happy. They feel good *and nobody (is around) to stop them from doing what they want* [Italics added].

10 "Different religious denomination," includes changes between denominations within a larger religion.

In this scene, pride isn't about accomplishment or innate self-esteem. Rather it's about freedom to do what you want, even if it conflicts with what other people think you ought to be doing. Pride and humility are linked, each concept at least partly defined by its contrast to the other. Therefore, if pride is connected to doing your own thing, humility is connected to living up to social expectations.

Another recent study shows the new world retains vestiges of the old. Michelle N. Shiota and other psychologists developed a set of five questions to measure people's pride in themselves. This measure asked people to what extent they agreed with these five statements: (1) "I feel good about myself," (2) "I am proud of myself and my accomplishments," (3) "Many people respect me," (4) "I always stand up for what I believe," and (5) "People usually recognize my authority."

In constructing this type of scale, researchers come up with a long list of potential questions and have people answer them. Then, researchers use a statistical analysis to select a few of those questions (in this case five) that are extremely closely related to each other, in that a person who says "yes" to any one of the questions is very likely to say "yes" to all the others. In fact, the relationship between the questions must prove to be so strong that all the questions are really getting at the same underlying thing.

It's not surprising that the first three questions (feel good about myself, proud of accomplishments, and many people respect me) are all just differently worded ways of asking about pride. But it is much more surprising that the last two questions—about standing up for what you believe and having other people recognize your authority—were shown in a statistical analysis to also be different ways of asking about pride. It seems that even today, pride still contains elements that work against obedience to the powers that be. But now these traits are re-cast as virtues.

If you look again at the graphs showing the plummeting usage of the terms "humility," "humble," and "pride," you may notice a slight uptick in usage of these terms starting around 1990. Though small, we hope this uptick reflects a renewed interest in the topic. For, despite acknowledging humility's darker side, we desperately need a reconstructed and reinvigorated notion of humility today.

The move from "stay in your place" to "pursue your dreams" is a big step forward for society. Part of this change was the idea that, as we pursue our dreams, we should trust our inner voice and our intuition, above all else. In many ways this is a good thing, but today we have too much of that good thing. For example, if you ask group members to gauge their contribution to a group accomplishment, the reported contributions almost inevitably exceed one hundred percent. Why? Subjectively, the work we did on the project feels very substantial because we experienced every minute of it, and we don't experience other people's work the same way. So, it truly does feel to us that we did more than our share, which leads us to become self-righteous and resentful. Writ large, everyone overvaluing themselves and undervaluing others is not a recipe for a happy community. When our intuition tells us that we did more than our share, we need to trust it less.

Movies often tell the stories of emotionally insecure protagonists who finally learn to disregard all the evidence and instead trust their gut, which turns out (always) to be right. But in real life, our guts are often full of excrement. Trusting yourself is often indistinguishable from believing anything that makes you feel good about yourself, which is a modern version of the sin of pride. Proponents of simply "trusting yourself" would do well to remember that all of the Klansmen and white supremacists that marched in Charlottesville in 2017 were trusting their intuitions and "speaking their truth." Similarly, when people believe that vaccines cause autism or that millions of people voted illegally for Joe Biden in the 2020 election, they too are trusting their inner voice over what "the experts" have to say.

Our point is not that listening to one's intuition is evil or always misleading, but that we need to be better at deciding if listening to one's inner voice is the right thing to do. We suggest two rules of thumb.

First, if your gut is telling you something that makes you feel superior to someone else, watch out. This includes feeling morally superior to someone else because they are an evil aggressor and you are an innocent victim. We stress that in real life this does happen. The Africans who were kidnapped and brought to America as slaves were undeniably innocent victims of a truly evil aggressor. But when our spouse gets angry at us for not cleaning up (even though they didn't clean up the day before!), both parties should exercise some humility and try to see things from the other's perspective.

Second, if the question is about oneself, listening to one's inner voice is essential; but if the question is about other people or the external world, your inner voice is more likely to get things wrong. Imagine you are choosing a career path. If the issue is what kind of work you enjoy, you should listen to your inner voice. But if the question is what kinds of skills will be in demand in the job market, you should look to outside sources of expertise. This example may make this rule of thumb seem obvious (at least we hope so), but in real life people frequently do make judgements about the external world based purely on how they feel.

Humility can make one aware of one's own shortcomings and, thus, less judgmental of others. It also promotes a mindset in which one is aware that even one's most emotionally gratifying beliefs might turn out to be wrong, and that the "nonsense" put forward by people who disagree with you might actually turn out to be right. In these ways, a dose of the proper humility can help us take another step forward.

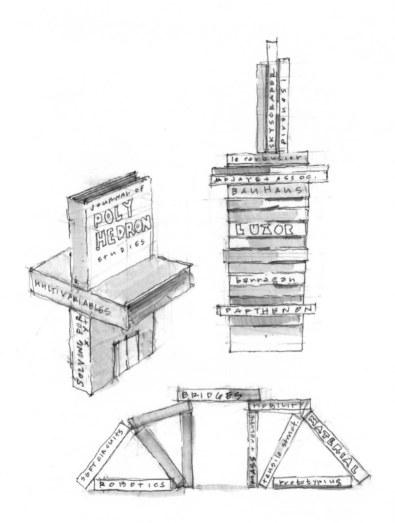

A LIBRARY IS FOR YOU

Jamie Vander Broek

When introducing the library, I often ask people to imagine themselves in a museum. Although they are both institutions that exist to preserve and share things, museums and libraries position themselves differently. Museums contain objects arranged in settings that elevate their perceived importance. Close your eyes and picture a museum. You might see uniformed guards and barriers to keep you at a safe distance from the items hanging on walls and displayed in glass vitrines. Probably you aren't picturing yourself physically interacting with the objects, unless you like to imagine yourself getting in trouble.

If, instead, you picture yourself in a library, your imagined experience is likely much different. Libraries recede into the background of a user's experience. Personal interactions with books and other media are foregrounded rather than the objects themselves. A museum is important. A library is for you.

I should maybe stop here and say that I don't have anything against museums. I worked at one in graduate school, and for a while I was convinced that I wanted to become an art museum librarian, a very niche and museum-loving sort of thing to do. In fact, even if I think of museums as positioned opposite libraries on a spectrum of humility and arrogance, sometimes arrogance can be a useful tool for institutions that are constantly under threat.

Museums are experts at trading in their perceived societal importance. The annual Met Gala, a benefit for the Metropolitan Museum of Art's Costume Institute, is a perfect example of this. Each spring, celebrities and socialites work to outdo one another in responding to the event's theme. The red carpet portion of the event now rivals the Academy Awards for media coverage, and it was even the centerpiece of the film *Ocean's 8.* According to the *New York Times*, in 2017, the event raised over $12 million.

Libraries look at these threats and adopt a different strategy. The library I work in is part of a system of over 11 million volumes. If you were patient enough, you could have personal access to every single one of those, from ancient sheets of papyrus to born-digital books that have never been released in print. This is why I say that libraries are for you. Both libraries and museums are concerned with preserving their holdings, and the inner workings of each contain people dedicated to this effort. But the public-facing parts of a museum are really not about their objects so much as a succession of *curators* interpreting and presenting their materials. As visitors, we see only the tip of the iceberg in terms of museum holdings; most of what they own is kept away from public view in carefully controlled storage areas. What you get to see is always through someone else's lens.

Libraries, instead, devote relatively little real estate and resources toward interpreting their collections, instead foregrounding the *individual's* experience with the materials. Another person's ego doesn't stand in the way of your access to, at our library, a letter handwritten by Galileo and the first cookbook published by an African American. That's how important you are to us.

Even if libraries contain rare, valuable, or one-of-a-kind resources, they usually don't exert much effort promoting these objects, particularly when compared to museums. They are obsessively concerned, by contrast, with providing pervasive access to all of their items. My library, for example, holds more writings on ancient papyrus than any other institution in the Western hemisphere. These objects are available literally nowhere else in the world. But you'd never know it when you walk in the door. Instead, you'll probably see information about the new version of our online catalog. In other words, who cares that some of the things we have are particularly special, even to many people? What really matters is that *you* can find what you're looking for.

Sometimes I make the mistake of attempting to visit a library as if it is a museum. Recently I traveled to Salt Lake City for a conference. The event offered tours of the Family History Library, which is the world's largest collection of genealogical materials. I eagerly signed up, but when I got there, I was surprised to find that it looked like, well, a library. There was a small interactive area much like the displays in a children's science museum, with opportunities for selfies with digital ancestors. But beyond that, there were stacks of regular-looking books and large cases of microfilm reels. I realized that because I hadn't prepared some questions about my own family, my time there was rather pointless, and I felt sheepish to have traveled such a long way to come to this conclusion as a professional librarian.

Some libraries, though, are more like museums to us, or at least hybrids. The New York Public Library's famous flagship branch on 42nd Street or the Library of Congress in Washington, D.C., for example. One could be forgiven for showing up at either of these locations without a research question, and in fact I have done just that at both. The leader of the latter institution is one of the few librarians people have (possibly) heard of: Librarian of Congress Carla Hayden. In an essay in the *New Yorker*, "The Librarian of Congress and The Greatness of Humility," Sarah Larson characterizes Hayden's mission in Washington D.C. as essentially to bring the lofty, museum-like institution back down to earth, aspiring to emulate the bustling, lively Baltimore Public Library system she used to direct. Explaining the massive Library of Congress facilities to readers, Larson suggests that, like Hayden, they embody a paradox of "greatness and humility—the interplay and tension between them, the importance of both—seemed to echo across each gleaming stairway and emanate from each carefully labelled acid-free folder." The greatness, the cathedral-like setting, and the sense that the institution is important even if most people don't understand what it does—these attributes make the Library of Congress a kind of hybrid museum-library, a vaunted status shared by only a few other libraries in the world. However, Hayden's service-driven mission reflects the dilemma of being valued without being relevant or particularly embedded in people's real lives.

One might ask whether the humble, unassuming attitude that most libraries adopt serves them very well. Libraries contain within themselves the most lofty ideals of a democratic society, but the average citizen would be hard-pressed to articulate that. We think of libraries as being about books or even literacy. But they're really about sharing. They're about recognizing the value of saving, sharing, and access to society. Public libraries, specifically, are civic organizations, representing the best of what our democratic model has to offer. Without reminders about their collectively boundless contents, are people very likely to think of libraries as places to seek answers, or even new questions, when faced with a blinking cursor in an empty search bar? To speak to the usefulness of a humble posture, I think we have to examine public libraries and research libraries separately.

I serve on our local public library's board of trustees. One of my former colleagues, who gave many years of his life to the board, often boasts that in all this time he has never checked out a book. He maintains his own large, personal library of rare and not-so-rare books. Why use the library when he has a perfectly good one of his own?, he asks. When talking about libraries with people outside my community, I often hear a related retort: why do we need libraries when everything is online and we can order what we need quickly and cheaply from Amazon? I see in these attitudes a community selling itself short, failing to consider the vast potential they have when working together to share something instead of investing in their own tiny empires.

Idealized self-reliance is at odds with the possibility of strength through cooperation. The self-reliant mindset romanticizes capitalism and its trappings, valuing acquisitions and demonstrations of accomplishment. The coronavirus pandemic exposed some of the weaknesses inherent in this behavior. No matter how much wealth or stuff a person might accumulate, there are some challenges that a community can only overcome together. In contrast, cooperation offers efficiencies that independence lacks. People can do more when they share their talents and efforts with each other, and research has demonstrated that diversity makes this especially true.

Our current age, though dominated by characters who champion self-reliance, is seeing a rise in library use. A new generation is using the library more than their parents. I would argue that younger people value sharing. They also have a reason to. Younger adults can't expect to own property at the same rate their parents did, and they are questioning ownership and the pride that comes from ownership. They are also challenging us to recognize the underlying equality of humans through movements like Black Lives Matter and Transgender Awareness.

A focus on community has served the public library well in a society in which young people are eschewing ownership. Even some who have amassed fortunes in the tech sector, for example, have walked away to live simpler lives less burdened by belongings. They thus become unexpected allies of people who have always depended on community—marginalized and disadvantaged populations. In our community, a recently renovated branch library with elegant, comfortable furniture and a cozy fireplace is an office for entrepreneurs working from home as well as a place to use a free computer and stay out of the elements. In holding steady to a model of sharing, the public library has become a cultural darling, hosting standing-room only sushi demonstrations and Bob Ross painting events, despite echoes of doom still ringing in the ears of those who preached a model of everyone for themselves.

Academic or research libraries are a little different. While they have also ridden out the wave of projected irrelevance, their essential organizational humility has prevented them from fully capitalizing on the current moment. At academic libraries, we lack shrewdness and have had a hard time putting aside our commitment to service to develop and advance a strategy. The same spirit that leads us to equally obsess over the family photographs of Orson Welles on vacation in the Alps and the most recent edition of a math textbook makes us ill-equipped for success in contemporary life. Beyond the energy we pour into making our collections available to you, we can get so caught up in the needs of our users that we forget to have ideas of our own, or when we do we aren't quite sure how to make them come to life.

As a product of these two library environments, I personally exemplify these tensions. I've been working on the project that led to this book for several years. Throughout my experience, I've struggled to conceptualize what I could add to it as a librarian. We were pulling together experts from academic disciplines, artists, a lawyer, a business leader—what sort of voice did I have to lend? I wasn't sure. I was so used to helping other people effectively find things, briefly attending to their journeys as they prepared, created, and shared their thoughts, that I didn't see how I might occupy anything but negative space in the product of our collaboration. Much like a doula, I was used to offering support but not to ownership. It was never my baby.

As I read a version of this essay to the gathered speakers at the colloquium on humility, I was struck, however, by the attention and participation of my audience. Rather than looking bored with a talk on humility and libraries, as I feared they might be, they seemed to be synthesizing the perspective I was sharing with their own lifelong experiences with libraries, now considering them in a slightly different way. I realized that there was power in the ability of individuals to make libraries thoroughly their own in their minds. Even if you are more comfortable in the background, it's ok to speak up when you really have something to say.

There is probably a lesson here about the potential power of adopting a humble orientation as a strategy. If you're all about everyone else's aspirations, perhaps others can continue to focus on themselves when working with you, which is probably what they prefer to be doing in the first place. But one can see quickly the potential pitfalls of this mode of operation. It can be too easy to seek comfort in receding into the background and allowing others to shine. Perhaps this is why librarians are notoriously quiet, shy people?

Libraries could consider borrowing a little of the arrogance of museums, if only for the sake of advancing their cause and broadcasting it to a larger audience. But I think the lesson here is that they don't need to. Institutional humility has allowed people to make libraries exactly what they need them to be. Their power, which can never be matched by organizations more focused on status and self-promotion, is in their authentic connection to individuals, in service to the journeys in their minds. Libraries offer both a mirror of one's interests and limitless, individualized paths to explore new territory. Imagine yourself in a library. Where will you go today?

HUMUS AND
THE HUMBLE LEADER

Kevin Hamilton

umility is not a trait we often associate with leaders. The very idea of a "humble leader" presents a contradiction. When we follow someone, don't they grow larger, acquire new authority and renown? Humble acts *give* the stage, where leaders typically rise through *taking* the stage. Even the practice of "servant leadership," popularized within management circles, strains to make room for humility; the word makes no appearance in *The Servant as Leader*, Robert Greenleaf's influential essay that launched the idea in 1970.

The spare mention of humility in Greenleaf's work offers some helpful clues to understanding why humility struggles to find a place in modern leadership. His worthy explorations of leading through servanthood certainly offered countless managers reason to put the care and well-being of employees and colleagues above their own individual advancement. But Greenleaf's idea of the servant-leader also leaves in place many of the structures and systems for which humble leadership represents a threat.

The servant-leader, Greenleaf writes, serves by taking on the problems they see in the world as "his or her own personal task, a means of achieving his or her own integrity."[11] They begin with caring for others to "help them grow and become healthier, stronger, and more autonomous."

11 Greenleaf, R. K. (1970). *The Servant as Leader.* Robert K. Greenleaf Publishing Center.

In relying on this social ideal of free-thinking individuals, Greenleaf also eschews "systems, ideologies, and movements" as insufficient to dealing with "the massive problems of our times."

This picture of service presents dependence as weak, and independence as strong. In Greenleaf's view, care for others reinforces the servant-leader's own position, and stands to create future leaders who do the same. This does not sound to me like the change we need among our leaders, and reminds me of why I believe leadership today calls for humility in the first place. Humility, in my understanding, is no mere prioritization of others above self, but rather a deeper subjection of self to others—a change that transforms the boundaries of the self. Humility calls for the surrendering of boundaries, an invitation to others to play a determining role in my life. True humility reduces my own independence and autonomy. As such, humility should also raise questions when espoused as a value, given how many start out with little independence to surrender in the first place.

Understood as an invitation to surrender autonomy, humility presents a challenge to anyone paying attention to that "massive problem" of systemic racism. For if humility represents a posture of vulnerability and surrender, what are we to call the "forced humility" of slavery and colonial violence that forms the bedrock of contemporary life in America? As a descendant of white settlers and slaveowners, my opportunity to choose humility—to willingly subject myself to others as a sovereign individual—comes at the cost of that opportunity stolen from others. Like my father before me and my sons after me, I am a "born leader," with a choice about whether to be humble about it, just as others are born never expecting to see an invitation to self-sufficiency and autonomy.

Humility thus struggles to find a role in leadership because in this society and nation, built on slavery and the production of autonomy and self-sufficiency for white people (and white men in particular), a leader subjecting herself or himself to others represents a threat to the social order. Because I share the view that our current dominant social order, built on the criminalization of Black and Brown bodies, requires thorough dismantling, I consider humility a practice to which leaders of our most prominent institutions are uniquely called. If collective organizing represents one way of transforming our institutions of business, education, health, and government, humble leadership is another. Until revolution transforms us all, we will need both.

I offer this perspective from within the industry wherein Robert Greenleaf incubated his servant-leader ethos (after leaving a long executive career at AT&T)—that of higher education. My path to the deanship I currently hold illustrates how the creation of leadership opportunities for some comes at the cost of denied opportunities to others. My ability to choose humility as an approach to leadership is directly contingent on the imposition of humility on others.

To tell this story, I have to go back to 2007. That was the year when, after close to a century of reliance on a racist "Indian chief" mascot in the advancement of community pride, identity, and alumni donations, the University of Illinois, Urbana-Champaign, where I work, finally conceded to requests from the National Collegiate Athletic Association to retire the popular symbol. In the wake of this decision, university leaders began to prioritize the hiring of new faculty in American Indian Studies—both to address the harm to native faculty and students who had endured a torrent of hatred from fans loyal to the old mascot, and to repair the university's soiled national reputation.

In universities, new faculty positions are among the most precious of resources. So this gesture represents, on the surface, an appropriate address of past wrongs. Yet in this case—as others have pointed out about hiring to race and ethnic studies program—this accrual of talent also came with unique new calls on faculty labor that few other professors faced. The university needed new American Indian Studies faculty not only to teach, but to bear the burden of helping this predominantly white university demonstrate as "inclusive" and reformed.

This position—that of the oppressed who nonetheless receive "gifts" that obligate them to service—is a familiar one from slavery and colonization. As in the trope of the "friendly Indian" within mythologies of the American West, or even the Uncle Tom figure from the Jim Crow era , we see here a kind of forced humility—a posture of service that may present as voluntary, but which serves those in power. In the years that followed, this would bear out in catastrophic ways when native faculty refused to take up such a role.

The university's spate of conciliatory hiring reached its zenith in 2013 with the hires of Joy Harjo, a Muscogee artist, writer, and eventual poet laureate of the United States, and Steven Salaita, a Palestinian-American scholar whose internationally-recognized scholarship applied histories of colonization to understanding Israel's role in Palestine. In an unprecedented move, university leaders rescinded Salaita's offer of employment, after his views and speech on behalf of Palestinians reached the ears of influential donors. The ensuing furor earned native faculty a renewed round of hatred and explicit threats to their safety. It also earned the University of Illinois a high-profile censure by America's highest oversight body for higher education, and the resignation of at least two high-ranking executives.

The vacancies created by these resignations resulted in a predictable leadership shuffle—and my first entry into a formal leadership role. I took my first regular position in the Dean's office after our dean rose to take one of the roles vacated through resignation. From there, my path to the deanship became almost inevitable; within a few short years I became the obvious (to many) appointee to one of the highest positions in the university, without ever having sought or applied for the role. Meanwhile, Steven Salaita found himself in economic precarity, plagued by the Illinois episode in a way that would make a future in higher education impossible. Today, he drives a school bus for a living. And most of the outstanding scholars hired to American Indian Studies during that time fled this university, "cleared" as thoroughly as their ancestors during white settlement. Those who stayed, like their Black and Brown colleagues, continue to face challenges to their work and life.

The story of Steven Salaita's fall and my attendant rise demonstrates not only the risks of stepping outside of such a position of forced humility, but how my freedom as a leader to *choose* humility comes directly from the denial of that choice to others. If humility among leaders like myself is essential to dismantling such processes, and yet even the most prominent examples of humble leadership leave this unequal distribution of forced humility unexamined, where am I to go to find models and examples for my work? My search for answers to this question took me to humility's etymological cousin *humus*—a word we often associate with earth or soil.

There are many kinds of earth and soil, but colloquially, humus refers to the completely decomposed organic material found in the layers beneath our feet. It's the dark stuff, best known to composters, and alternately described as "spongy" or even "jelly-like." If we were to go into a forest and sweep back the layer of fallen leaves, then dig just a little below the surface, we'd find what the leaves of past seasons had become—a rich, dark layer of moist earth.

Scientists and farmers have struggled with understanding exactly what goes on in that layer of earth, and how it supports life. The current theory is that when living things decay, micro-organisms eat away at what they can of the formerly living matter, transferring minerals from that material into the roots of plants. What's left over—what those micro-organisms can't eat—becomes a kind of skeleton for the whole process, and for future processes. This skeleton of undigestible material retains water, and provides a physical structure for the process of mineral extraction that microorganisms help along through consumption and waste.

Living things thus become humus when the lively microscopic organisms in the soil have sufficiently fed on our remains, so that we can then provide a structure for others—a hospitable home for these little animals that keep the process going. As humus, formerly living things provide a place for plants to take root, a scene for the breaking down of future life into usable materials. Humus is a kind of architecture, a structure that gets out of the way to let life happen. Water, light, and minerals find their way to organisms by taking up space a once-living being left behind.

We owe this picture of humus largely to an underrecognized ecologist named Annie France-Harrar. She wrote passionately and knowledgeably about not only the processes taking place in this lively interplay of living and dead matter, but also about the dependence of the very planet on healthy humus. Anticipating many a contemporary ecologist, she saw threats to humus as threats to all life. Foresting, mining, and agriculture practices that don't leave time for decomposition would, through erosion, impoverish and weaken the very ground beneath our feet.

"Until now our civilization and culture have been built on a large scale devastation of humus," Francé-Harrar wrote in her 1950 book *The Last Chance: for a Future Without Need.* "Man is now no more than a chronic disturber of humus cycles."[12]

In her view, through degradation of the humus layer, the very surface of the earth had become unstable. She wrote about examples of this with breathtaking mobility, bouncing from continent to continent to describe the special and unique ways in which humanity had imperiled the planet through loss and destruction of soil life. Francé-Harrar loved the process of humification, and brought particular love for the rhizomatic plants, vines, grasses, indeed even the kudzu of my southern youth, for the ways in which these beings grew fast and died, easily contributing to the process of life.

I love this picture of humus in which, across the planet, the dead don't simply feed the living, but invite them in to reside in their very selves. Within the context of Francé-Harrar's call for the replenishment of humus, I imagine a planet of "born leaders" surrendering autonomy to become porous, inviting others in to take root and flourish. The structures of leadership as we know them, historically dependent on theft from others, can die to provide the structure in which new forms take life.

What might this mean in my day-to-day work as a leader in a predominantly white institution? How might I contribute to the slow death of the role I inhabit—not just to feed a different role as Steven Salaita's stolen position made new room for me in mine, but to provide a fertile architecture in which

12 Francé-Harrar, Annie (1950). *Die letz Chance für eine Zukunft ohne* Not. München Bayer.

others can imagine whole new ways of living interdependently? Now in my third year as dean, I'm working on this daily, and focused on how humus creates room inside itself, becomes "sponge-like," full of holes and voids.

If I remove the words *I* might have used to guide a public conversation, *whose* words might take their place? As the agent responsible for many a decision-making body, what if I were to invite another to set the agenda? What decisions left to me can I expose to others on a regular basis, providing them the information and knowledge provided to me, and carrying out their conclusions? How can I, in my role as leader, not only serve others but follow the path of humus, of humility, to invite others in to my very self? And how can I help ensure that once I've helped make room for other life, the process continues after I'm gone?

I've even begun to consider the dimensions of my role that bear the most benefit to me personally, to see what space I can carve out there. If I accept that change will take many years to complete, and stay put to see it happen rather than angling for a better position, what space opens up for the matters and concerns unique to my current community to take hold of me? Might there even be room for others within the very monetary compensation I receive for the work? Could I carve a new space there as well, inviting others to claim a piece of my inflated salary for application in ways beyond the bestowing of prestige and value?

To be clear, revolution will not take place on the terms of "born leaders," humble or not. Fires are also important to soil replenishment, and there are quite a few burning in the fields I steward. But while the revolution wages, if anyone finds herself in a position of leadership within a historically white institutions and wonders what she can do, let them take a lesson from humus. Let us make room in ourselves for others, becoming a rich new layer of structure in which others can rise. And when we leave these roles behind, may we find both ourselves and the positions we held profoundly and mercifully changed.

to prevent harm

THE SOUL OF MEDICINE

Richard C. Boothman

L et me tell you two stories. One about Christine and one about Ahmad. Christine was a vibrant seventy-two-year-old woman who began to have headaches and then a dizzy spell. A CT scan ordered by her physician showed a congenital problem in her brain, called an arteriovenous malformation. There was an unusual juncture between her cerebral arteries and veins, and it posed a risk for bleeding and rupture. So, her physicians performed a really cool procedure in which they placed a catheter in her groin threading it through her body up to the little spot in her brain, and then they embolized, or clotted it off. They didn't have to cut her skull open, they didn't have to mess with her brain, but there are still obvious risks with this.

The procedure went beautifully, but in the middle of the night her nurses noted that one side of her face was drooping and her grip strength was diminished, worrisome suggestions that she had suffered a stroke of some sort. The chief resident in neurosurgery called the attending physician at home and explained the situation, and they hatched a plan: rush Christine down to the CAT scanner. If the neuroradiologist saw signs of a bleed, they would get her directly into the operating room and drain the blood. And if there were no signs of a bleed, it was probably a clot, in which case they would give her heparin, a powerful anticoagulant, and see if they could restore her circulation. Great plan. So, the resident summoned two experienced surgical intensive care nurses and said, "get me 3,000 units of heparin and come with me." They ran down in the middle of the night to the CAT scanning unit and determined there was no sign of a bleed. They administered the heparin, and she improved dramatically for about forty minutes, and then she crashed. An emergency scan revealed a dramatic new intracerebral bleed, so large it was deemed inoperable.

I'll tell you later what happened to Christine, but first I want to tell you about Ahmad.

Ahmad was a tall, twenty-eight-year-old Syrian son of immigrant parents. In the fall of 2010, he started having unexplained nosebleeds. He was seen by a community hospital a couple of times, and every time he would go in, they would say "you've got nosebleeds, go back to your primary care doc." So, he would do just that. He repeated this cycle several times until he showed up in the University of Michigan emergency room in June of 2011 in serious trouble. His lips were blue. He struggled to get air and the emergency physicians were unable to stop the profuse bleeding now coming from his nose and mouth. Doctors took Ahmad to an exam room and started to investigate what was going on. While that was happening, ten members of his family assembled in the lobby. Nobody spoke English very well.

While Ahmad was in the back, the doctors first put a scope down his nose and airway. They saw active bleeding but couldn't see the source. They did an imaging study and they saw a big mass that could either be a tumor or a clot in his pulmonary artery. As three specialists began to discuss next steps, the clot in Ahmad's pulmonary artery eroded through the vessel wall. In four beats of his heart, Ahmad bled to death.

Minutes later, the doctors came out into the lobby to tell the family that Ahmad was dead. The family erupted. Furniture was broken. Death threats were made. The police were called. Ahmad's family was ushered off the premises without an opportunity to see his body. And I received a phone call, not about Ahmad's death, but about whether we wanted to press criminal charges against his family.

That's my world. This can happen on any given day for me. As first a trial lawyer and then the Chief Risk Officer for the University of Michigan Health System, I've spent nearly forty years immersed in these stories. The manner in which patients are treated after they are injured in the course of their medical care is complicated by competing concerns and cultures and by human nature. I will tell you what happened to Ahmad's family and to Christine, but first let me tell you about how we have changed things at Michigan.

Nobody goes into the business of healthcare for the money, in my opinion; it's far too rigorous a lifestyle and there are lots of ways to make more money easily. It's also personally taxing and emotionally taxing. Some might get cynical later in their career, but not originally. These are talented perfectionists, self-selected largely because they find meaning for themselves in helping others. The heavy mix of emotions they experience when something they have done goes wrong and a patient is harmed is enormous.

And though no caregiver enters the profession intending to hurt the patients who entrusted their lives to them, patients can be, and are hurt by avoidable medical mistakes. In its 1999 publication, *To Err is Human*, the Institute of Medicine estimated that nearly 100,000 Americans died as a result of medical errors; since, new publications report the real number of avoidable deaths may be four times the Institute's initial estimate. And this is happening in an environment that I have come to regard as fortress medicine.

It wasn't so long ago when we lived in an agrarian society, a time when, if you broke your arm on the farm, you were grateful that the doc would take the horse and buggy and come out and set your arm on the kitchen table. You owned one hundred percent of your healthcare and your problems at that time. Look how that's changed. Medicine started developing amazing expertise; after World War II, Medicine started building big hospitals and healthcare providers wearing inscrutable, intimidating white coats spoke in medical jargon that patients didn't understand, instead of reaching people where they really live. Pretty soon caregivers and administrators behaved as though they were doing patients a favor when they came to be seen. Medicine's reason for being should be the patient, but it doesn't feel that way anymore. They built a fortress with its waiting rooms and its own language and its own social systems and those in charge consider themselves enlightened when they use the buzzwords "patient engagement" and think to invite you in. Fortress medicine.

And in the process of losing sight of the patient, they too often elevated the financial concerns above all else. Lawyers like me got hired to handle the defense of cases like Christine's using a system that's aptly called "deny and defend." My governing mantra as a trial lawyer was, "If a defense could be made, the defense would be made."

But "deny and defend" hasn't worked very well for any of us. Predictably, patients feel betrayed. They feel abandoned. They are deeply embittered when, after entrusting their lives to the medical establishment, they find themselves alone dealing with new clinical realities when things go wrong. Nobody's talking to them, everybody is guarded and sometimes not honest. It is not unusual that, after an adverse event occurs, patients never see their doctor again.

When our daughter was in medical school, she called home the first time she was on a clinical rotation and she said, "Dad, I don't know if I can do this. I spent the whole day in rooms with people I don't know, who took their clothes off, who told me the most intimate parts of their lives, who let me put my hands on them ... who are looking to me to fix what's wrong with them. The responsibility is overwhelming." I remember saying to her, "Don't ever lose that. You've got to find a way to remember that sense of awe every single day of the rest of your career." And yet the bitter paradox with "deny and defend": healthcare works to establish the most intimate relationships between caregiver and patient and then turns on a dime the minute the patient gets hurt.

None of this works for caregivers, either. When a patient gets hurt, caregivers believe that they are the only ones who have ever made a mistake. There's a bitter, bitter mix of shame and fear. They're worried about their jobs. They're worried about their financial future. They're worried about their reputations. Many times, they don't even tell their families what's happened to them, partly because we've told them not to talk to anybody, partly because there are powerful emotions at work preventing them from telling even their loved ones.

For the first twenty-one years of my career, I represented health systems and care providers in medical malpractice cases. I was hired to defend the claims that arose from patient injuries. We counseled caregivers and health care organizations to abandon their mission in deference to ours: Circle the wagons. Don't say anything to the patient. Don't admit mistakes. Don't explain. Don't show compassion lest it be misconstrued as an admission of fault. We instructed them to turn away from their patients the minute the patient was hurt, the moment in time their patient needed help the most. The instructions we gave cut directly across the healthcare grain, and hospitals and caregivers largely obeyed. Partly because lawyers have an outsized impact in that healthcare community, partly because caregivers and healthcare administrators were privately relieved to have lawyers' permission to avoid the painful situation.

After being hurt in the course of their medical care and then stonewalled by the very people to whom they previously entrusted their lives, patients reported feeling betrayed, bewildered and abandoned; and, in the absence of an honest explanation, they hired lawyers. Deny and defend created the very problem it was intended to address: instead of avoiding litigation, we invited it. We pushed patients into litigation as the only avenue left to them, then labeled them "litigious" to justify our own stereotype.

More corrosive than litigation is the impact "deny and defend" has on the overall healthcare culture and consequently, on safety. A profoundly defensive environment is hardly conducive to the introspection required for progress. Clinical improvement freezes when we discourage change while we wait to see what will happen with a claim. Future patients continue to be placed at risk, which to me is the most ethically reprehensible part of it all. When we sublimate all concerns to self-preservation in the immediate situation, we put other people at risk day in and day out. Injured patients are seen as a cost of doing business in fortress medicine, the antithesis of what they were before they got hurt. Think about how incongruous that is. I did exactly that as a lawyer defending hospitals.

After years in practice I started to feel guilty. So in 2001, I left private law practice to try what seemed like a straightforward idea. I explained to my wife and my law partners that I was leaving the firm that I founded to do this experiment. The concept was pretty simple, and it was really based on what we would tell our kids: If you make a mistake, step up, be honest about it, and do your best to make it right. If you didn't make a mistake, explain yourself but don't let anyone take advantage of you. And for God's sake, learn from your experiences.

Christine. I learned about Christine at 6:00 in the morning when I had just arrived at the office. The chief resident was peering around the corner in tears. At that very moment, the attending surgeon, summoned from home, was meeting with sixteen members of Christine's family informing them that Christine was on life support solely to allow them a chance to say good-bye. The attending talked about the inherent dangers of heparin that caused Christine's complication, concluding that there was nothing he could offer aside from his deep sorrow and sincere condolences.

What the attending didn't know at that moment was that during the night, the chief resident had rummaged through medical waste and found the empty containers of heparin he had administered. His worst fears were realized. In the heat of the moment, in the middle of the night, he had seen 1,000 on each of the three vials. He had not noticed in smaller print, "x 10." He had administered 30,000 units of heparin, not 3,000. He was the only one who knew this and he was there to confess it to me.

The chart documented the appropriate 3,000 unit dose. The nurses thought they had provided the appropriate dose. The attending thought they had administered the correct dose. This could have happened with the correct dose. And now the attending surgeon was explaining to the family how the complication occurred with what he thought was the appropriate dose. But the chief resident knew otherwise. He showed up in my office, tears streaming down his face, and insisted that he tell the family the truth.

We introduced the resident to the family. Through his tears, he did his best to explain the mistake to the dumbstruck family who sat in stunned silence around Christine for what seemed to be an eternity. And then Christine's sister stood, crossed the room and embraced him. She said, "We have watched you, and you really care. Remember my sister, but don't you dare quit. You're going to do a lot of good for a lot of people in your career. Don't you dare quit." Amazing. I cannot imagine such generosity of spirit. Such forgiveness.

In a punitive and defensive culture, the chance that a resident would self-report a serious medical mistake that caused the death of his patient is sadly remote. Mistakes like this are far more likely to be buried in medical waste and inaccurate medical records. Deny and defend would advise caregivers, "Keep your head down, don't talk to anyone and see if they file suit." And any opportunity for protecting future patients are likewise buried.

Within twenty-four hours, we had emailed the entire organization. If you worked in the cafeteria or in housekeeping or in the operating room, you got an email that said this had happened. We removed heparin, loose in bins, from all but the most essential places, requiring caregivers to access it only through the pharmacy in the future. We put stop sign labels on the heparin that said (in essence) "pay attention, that's ten times that one thousand number."

And we were able to comfort Christine's family with reassurances that her death had meaning, that others were not likely to suffer from the same complication. We embraced the resident and the nurses—all three were given time off and counseling. They all made a mistake, a critical mistake but they were part of a system that set them up.

Here's what happened with Ahmad's family. After we heard about their outburst in the waiting room, complete with broken furniture, not only did we *not* think about criminal charges, we immediately realized, "That poor family thought he had only nosebleeds. How could they reconcile nosebleeds with his death?" So we asked them back in order to explain, even before we had the autopsy results. We took security precautions and arranged for Ahmad's five physicians to be present and prepared to walk the family through the clinical details. The family did what many do: without warning, they brought a lawyer with them, which was fine. It is not uncommon that a patient or family feels the need to even the playing field. As it turned out, I was grateful they did.

The first hour was pretty rocky. One member of the family, just beside himself, was so furious that he lashed out at all of us. The family's lawyer intervened: "Stop!" he said firmly. "Do you realize there's not another hospital in the country that would do what they're doing today? Show some respect and let them explain."

Five physicians all deeply affected by their inability to prevent this young man's death, most with tears in their eyes, took their turns and chronologically walked the family through what they did, why they did it, the autopsy results, and why Ahmad died. Strictly speaking, they weren't apologetic because they hadn't done anything wrong at all. They had inherited this problem that had been brewing in Ahmad's lungs for months. But they were unguardedly empathetic. By the end of the explanations, everyone was crying, and the family impulsively started hugging the doctors and consoling the physicians because they were so racked. They could reach that common humanity between them.

Even though there were no clinical errors in Ahmad's care, we learned something valuable in talking to this family. The only person in the waiting room the day Ahmad died was a clerk with, as it turned out, a disparaging attitude toward Arabs and electronic games on her computer. While the intense life and death drama played out and a young man was dying, she played solitaire on her computer. How disrespectful! It was hard to listen to Ahmad's family as they described their building rage around her insensitivity to one of life's most profound dramas, but it was so valuable to view this profound moment through their eyes. Shortly after hearing their story, we removed games from computers. The clerk was ordered to undergo sensitivity training. We would never have known any of these things had we followed the deny and defend trajectory.

Now, more than seventeen years later, I'm pleased to say that the University of Michigan has normalized these ideas. Honesty and transparency resonated with Michigan physicians and nurses almost immediately and now, it is simply understood that it's part of what it means to deliver health care at Michigan. Outside the University however, the response was decidedly different, and I was naively unprepared. Our approach was first publicized in an early-2004 newspaper article. After sharing the concept, the logic, and our experiences including early claims savings at a conference that year, a leading scholar followed me to the podium and declared that I would "singlehandedly bankrupt the University of Michigan Health System in five years or less." The president of the American Medical Association next labeled me "reckless"; he dramatically removed himself from my table at a luncheon after the conference. In a 2007 piece published in a leading healthcare journal, a group of famous scholars called the approach "an improbable risk management strategy" and predicted that widespread adoption of the approach would "shake" the "fragile foundation" of affordable health care in this country. A New York judge scolded me before an audience of 400 in 2008: "You should be ashamed of yourself for exploiting injured patients at their most vulnerable." A law school professor in Boston characterized our approach in 2011 as consistent with the concept of "cooling the mark out," the "mark" being the victim of a con game. To this day there is no evidence that honesty and transparency about medical injuries threatens modern medicine, but the belief persists as established fact and though more hospitals are adopting this approach, change continues to be impeded by fear and self-interest. Few in medicine will ever witness the acts of grace and generosity we've been privileged to experience so many times.

Human beings are amazingly resilient in the face of unspeakable tragedy, but it is especially cruel to deprive injured and grieving people of the basic facts from which they can try to make sense of what has happened to them or their loved ones. It is heartless to ignore the profound hurt that caregivers feel when their patients are harmed. Most hospitals in this country and around the world continue to allow the insurance and legal priorities to drive how they respond to patients injured in the course of their care, and consequently valuable opportunities to learn and improve are lost. But I think they lose something even more profound: the past seventeen years have been a lesson in humility. The human capacity for forgiveness and understanding takes my breath away. Patients and families are more forgiving than anyone ever believed. Caregivers' personal commitment and caring is boundless when they know it's safe to confront their limitations and mistakes and express their feelings. The soul of medicine resides in people, simple and complex, but all capable of soaring acts of generosity if only given the chance. We are all humbled by the experience.

ADMITTING WHAT YOU DON'T KNOW IS HARD TO DO

Eranda Jayawickreme

I enjoy talking to strangers when I'm travelling. This might be because I'm a psychologist, or because I always try to look for the best in people, or perhaps it's a reflection of the fact that a dear family friend christened me "Tigger" when I was a child because of my apparently rampant extraversion. Regardless, whether it's in a cab, on a plane, or at a party, I'm likely to be the one happily chatting away with people I've never met before and will perhaps never see again. I've received primers on the history of tobacco in North Carolina, been subjected to multiple attempts at conversion by practitioners of various religions, discussed the question of whether all languages are in fact governed by universal laws, and been complimented as apparently "one of the good ones" (I try not to overthink that one now).

I take particular joy when they ask me what I do for a living. I always give them the same answer: I study happiness. They usually find this hilarious and tell me either that it suits my personality (a compliment?) or ask me what the keys to happiness are (I usually go with having close relationships, or not sweating the small stuff).

However, if I'm being honest I'm not telling them the truth about what I study. Well, it's not the whole truth. I study how we can live good lives. That is—how we can live lives of happiness, meaning, and purpose by successfully overcoming the challenges, failures, and adversity that are defining features of our lives, and how can we successfully develop into the best version of ourselves. The good life is not simply about feeling happy, but also doing things of value, feeling some control over your life, and—crucially for what I'll be discussing below—figuring out what's true about our world.

These days, I tend to think that perhaps the most important key to living well is the ability to see and understand both yourself and the world for what it really is. Understanding the world as it really is involves having: a) an accurate sense of oneself, and b) insight into what we can and cannot control. Doing this is much harder that you'd think. We as individuals routinely believe that we're better than average on pretty much any conceivable trait or ability. Many of us who grew up in cultural settings that prioritize individual choice and action further believe that we are masters of our universe and that we can bend our environment to meet our desires. This belief typically decreases as we age and are subjected to multiple life lessons that teach us the importance of luck in our lives.

Seeing the world for what it really is a form of wisdom. But it turns out that being wise is very hard. We each have our own biases (towards our own preferred in-groups, our families, our countries, our ideological commitments) that often shield us from the truth of the matter. Are there traits of character that we can develop to ensure that we understand the world the way it is?

I think intellectual humility may be one such trait. Being intellectually humble involves understanding your cognitive limitations—in simpler terms, it means acknowledging that you could be wrong about something. If you're not open to acknowledging that you could be wrong, you can't learn anything new about the world; you're not going to be able to change your beliefs and grow. As a human being, you probably intuit that this is a very hard thing to do. Try being intellectually humble when you're trying to convince your fiancée of the merits of inviting everyone we know to our wedding (for example). You have your own strong views, and your instinct is to fight for the one you happen to be in. Even if you know at the back of your mind that you'll regret it later (since you actually know very little about wedding planning or planning anything for that matter), and perhaps even know that she was right (the smaller, family-focused wedding she argued for ended up being perfect).

It turns out that there is some evidence that backs up this intuition. In a study we ran a few years ago, we asked college students twice a day for three weeks if they had exhibited the thoughts, feelings, and behaviors characteristic of intellectual humility in an argument with someone over the previous twelve hours. The students then rated the extent to which they sought out reasons for why their current opinions could be wrong and used new information to reevaluate their existing beliefs. It turns out that they were more likely to manifest this humility in situations where they saw the person they were arguing with as moral and therefore trustworthy. Conversely, they were less likely to deploy it in situations where they found the interaction to be disagreeable. Interestingly, the content of the disagreement—morality, facts, personal opinions—didn't have an impact on the degree of intellectual humility. More important was what the speaker thought of their interlocutor.

What does it mean to be intellectually humble when it counts? I don't know, to be honest (See what I did there?). But perhaps one way forward is to be mindful of how easily we can slip into defensiveness when we get into arguments, given that we all too easily see critiques of our understanding as critiques of our character. If we can remind ourselves of this tendency, perhaps we can find a way to remind ourselves that our interlocutors are not bad people, and that we can disagree without being disagreeable. This is a hard task, especially in the current political climate, as engaging with people we disagree with in this manner takes trust, curiosity, and open-mindedness. As I alluded to above, I've learned a lot from my fellow passengers on my travels—not only new insights in areas outside my expertise, but also how other Americans outside a university setting understand and approach their world. These conversations have not always been easy, and I have confronted my limits at times. For example, while I think I generally handle comments that are arguably prejudiced with some degree of grace, I have recently found debating with anti-vaxxers to be an impossible task. Understanding the world involves understanding the perspectives that others bring to it, and this requires both patience and skill that can sometimes be difficult to muster.

One key challenge, I think, is remaining intellectually humble and open-minded as you grow older and develop (reasonably justifiable) beliefs about your own competence and abilities. For example, as a psychologist with what I believe to be a deep understanding of the research on well-being and personality, as well as a broader appreciation of the scientific method and scientific thinking, I unconsciously approach most conversations that touch on these topics with an "expert" mindset. However, Socrates taught us many years ago that "knowing oneself" involved interrogating one's claims to knowledge, and that true knowledge may in fact involve a deep recognition of one's ignorance. In a way, gaining knowledge also involves dealing with the curse of knowledge—that complacent feeling that you've got it all figured out. In academia, I've found that increasing seniority is typically met with deference and occasionally (unwarranted) veneration. As the classicist Edith Hall noted in a recent talk, remaining critical of one's own ideas and open-minded to other's views in such a context takes some pretty significant—and constant—effort. Both our psychology and our contexts make admitting what we don't know very hard. We care about fitting in with family and friends, maintaining our ideological commitments and feeling good about ourselves, all of which make facing up to the truth challenging. But I think we are also creatures that care about the truth. Caring about the truth involves being vulnerable about what we don't know, and inhabiting such a state can be unnerving. However, I think that taking such chances in our daily lives is key to achieving the good life.

DON'T BE A KNOW-IT-ALL: OR, HOW TO BE A BETTER FRIEND

Valerie Tiberius and Melissa Koenig

Anyone who has read Jane Austen's novel *Emma*, or who has seen one of the many movies, will be familiar with a character named Mrs. Elton. Mrs. Elton is the wife of the local vicar and when she comes on the scene of the little village where Emma lives, she immediately attempts to befriend everyone and help them out. This seems nice! But the way that Mrs. Elton helps people is by doing what she sees as helpful, given her own ideas, without making the slightest effort to think about how things are from the point of view of the person she is "helping." Her plans to help her friend Jane Fairfax amount to frustrating everything Jane actually wants: Jane wants to walk to the post office alone while Mrs. Elton insists on accompanying her; Jane does not want to apply for positions as a governess, and Mrs. Elton finds a position for her immediately, and so on.

As a result, Mrs. Elton is overbearing and arrogant despite her good intentions. She thinks she knows best, when actually she has given very little attention to Jane's life, goals, and plans. Mrs. Elton has her ideas about what is good for Jane Fairfax (and everyone else in the town) that are based on her own upbringing in a high-society family. Mrs. Elton thinks that a woman of her status can hope to make a good match (that

127

is, find a rich husband), but a woman of lower social status like Jane must satisfy herself with taking care of someone else's children. As it turns out (spoiler alert), Jane is destined to make a very good match indeed, because she is secretly engaged to Frank Churchill. Frank's nasty aunt opposes the match, which is why it must be kept a secret until the aunt finally dies. Mrs. Elton has no clue about any of this and is not responsive to the gentle pressure Jane exerts to get Mrs. Elton to leave her alone.

Mrs. Elton is a know-it-all. She acts on her prejudices about women who are not quite in her class and she refuses to try to see things from someone else's point of view. She has little capacity to doubt her own opinions about anything. She insists on her views to the detriment of those around her. Mrs. Elton is a clear case of someone lacking in humility.

The kind of humility she sorely needs has two mutually reinforcing elements: (1) acknowledgement of the limited importance of her own point of view and (2) owning her limitations.

Let's talk about these two elements in a little more detail. The first thing about people with humility is that they understand that their own outlook is just one point of view among many. They do not take themselves to be the center of the universe (hence some researchers call this aspect of humility "de-centeredness").

The second thing about people with humility is that they take responsibility for their flaws and limitations. People who own their limitations realize that they have them and are inclined to improve upon them where they can. Owning our limitations is very important to being able to see things from a friend's point of view. We need to recognize that we don't know everything and that our capacity for understanding someone else's perspective is limited by our imagination, experience, assumptions, and our own values. Responding appropriately to what we know about what we don't know (that is "owning") means (at least) not assuming that you know what's best for others, being open to other new sources of information, and having forbearance with respect to any inclination to be overly critical, judgmental, or domineering.

In Mrs. Elton's case we can see that her lack of humility is bad for her friendships: people don't like her and she isn't very helpful. One problem with know-it-alls like this is that they do not bother to find out what is important to their friends, because they believe they already know what is good for them. And this leads to know-it-alls doing things and saying things they think are helpful that are actually harmful.

If you reflect on your own experience with friends and family members, our guess is that you will recall some experiences with know-it-alls trying to help. It's not helpful to have someone try to convince or coerce you into doing something that ignores what you think you need in life. This will be familiar to many people who have experienced "inter-generational advice." Members of older generations often think they know what's best and give advice to the younger generation without trying to understand what things are like for them, at which point the younger generation feels ignored and so doesn't listen. Many of us have been on both sides of this phenomenon! When friends do this to us it undermines the friendship because we end up feeling like they don't really care about *us*. After all, they don't care enough to find out what we're really like or to respect what we think and feel.

If we think of other examples of people who take their own outlook to be paramount and never doubt that they are right, we see how a lack of humility can become a problem on a larger social scale. For example, in the "Me Too" era, we have learned that men who cannot understand how things are from a woman's perspective, can do serious harm to the women they encounter. And people who have unexamined racial or religious prejudices hurt others in various ways without having any idea that they're doing it. When we do not acknowledge the limits of our knowledge about what things are like for other people, we are at risk of hurting people and damaging our relationships. This risk presents an obvious reason for us to try to cultivate humility.

For those of us who want to cultivate humility, then, a major barrier is our tendency to see our own opinions, and the opinions of those similar to ourselves, as beyond reproach, and to refuse to doubt them—just like Mrs. Elton, who could not see past the prejudices of her class. Where do these tendencies come from? In the last fifteen years or so, research in the field of child development shows that the capacity to doubt *other* people's communication emerges without training, very early in development, and even in families that cultivate deference. Psychologists at the Institute of Child Development at the University of Minnesota have presented hundreds of infants and children with terrible sources of information—speakers whose claims are false across a range of conditions—and measured kids' responses. Even by sixteen months of age, infants are surprised by false information, staring at such speakers longer than those who speak truthfully. Infants occasionally interrupt and overtly correct these false claims. At the same time, research has shown that children's learning is biased in favor of certain sources. Children (and adults, actually) often favor members of their own groups, and prefer to learn from those who are familiar, dominant, attractive, and from those who speak in ways that are similar to them.

So, we are born with the capacity to doubt, but we tend

to favor people who are familiar or similar to us in various ways over those who are less familiar or similar to us. For parents who want to raise children who think independently and without excessive bias, we think these observations recommend two things.

First, that children and adults become more deeply involved and acquainted with people who at first seem less familiar or similar to them. By expanding the reaches of one's own experience in relationship with others, others' lives and values become better understood through shared experiences and shared testimony. This isn't always easy to do, of course, but parents can look for opportunities to get out of their comfort zones and bring their children with them. Parents can pay attention to diversity when choosing sports programs, volunteer activities, or schools for their kids, for example.

Second, that children would benefit from seeing the familiar members of their families and communities—parents, teachers, family, clergy, political leaders—admit to the limits of their experience and knowledge, openly discuss their limits and mistakes, profess their doubts and make their uncertainty clear. The children of parents who model uncertainty and doubt will trust that this is a good way to be, imitate the behaviors, and will be more likely to develop humility.

This advice might run counter to a parent's first instinct, which is to teach their children all that they know about the world. But in fact, children may be much better served by conversations that combine a gift of nature (children's capacity for doubt) with our human limitations (limitations in knowledge and experience). By openly discussing our doubts and mistakes with children on a daily basis, we honor their deep concern for the truth, while modeling and practicing the skills that will help them develop their own values, the scope of their concern, and tools to seek out the truth independently.

At the time of this writing, discussions of racial injustice and the COVID-19 pandemic are taking place in families everywhere. Here, parents' tendencies to reassure children are understandable, but there is room for humility. A white parent might say, "I might not understand everything about the protests, because I don't know what it's like to be Black in this country. Why don't we find a book to read together that's written by a Black American?" On the pandemic, parents can reassure that we are doing everything to keep the family safe without pretending to be virologists or epidemiologists (a temptation the authors have noticed in themselves lately). Nor does modeling humility always have to be so high stakes. When children ask questions about why penguins are birds even though they can't fly, or why the sky is blue, parents can admit they don't know and offer to help find out.

Of course, openly discussing our own doubts and mistakes requires owning our limitations, which brings us back to humility in adults. For Mrs. Elton, and the rest of us, it's too late to ask our parents to model humility. What can we do as grown-ups? Can friends model and encourage humility for each other? Can we gain perspective on the significance of our own point of view in the grand scheme of things? Can we take greater ownership of our limitations?

One thing we can do is to consider strategies that will help to counteract the tendencies to think that we are always right and that our viewpoint is more important than anyone else's. We can see one good strategy by paying attention to a different character in *Emma*, namely, Emma. Like Mrs. Elton, Emma starts out very certain of her own opinions about what other people ought to do. But unlike Mrs. Elton, Emma is open to learning about herself from feedback, particularly from her trusted friend Mr. Knightly. Emma learns from Knightly that her arrogance hurts other people and she sets herself to making changes. What if one of Mrs. Elton's friends or sisters had suggested to her that she's kind of a know-it-all? What if a sister had shared an experience she had of alienating friends by being overbearing, and expressed her regret about this? Perhaps this would plant a seed of doubt in Mrs. Elton's head that caused her to take a pause when someone refuses her help, so that she can consider how much evidence she has that her help is wanted. She would not have to possess humility already in order to adopt this strategy. She might think "I'm usually right. But I trust my sister and I should consider her advice and experience. I might—albeit very rarely—be wrong".

Or, what if Mrs. Elton had adopted a strategy of imagining an alternative possibility whenever she found herself inclined to act on her beliefs about what's going on in someone else's life? Perhaps motivated by a sermon on walking a mile in someone else's shoes, she commits herself to a policy of dreaming up one alternative explanation for a friend's situation besides the one that comes immediately to her mind. She might think to herself: "What is another reason Jane might refuse my lift to the post office? Is it possible she prefers to walk? I hate walking, but I suppose it is possible there might be people who like it." Granted, these strategies may not help that much if Mrs. Elton is so arrogant that she can never recognize a situation in which she might be mistaken about something. But they may help over the long term, and no strategy will work for everyone.

Other strategies for cultivating humility in ourselves or in our children include setting your mind to asking friends at least one question about themselves before giving advice, admitting to your children you don't know something at least once a day, monitoring yourself to see if you've been judgmental without knowing the facts, or finding regular opportunities to interact with people who are outside of your familiar circle of family and friends. The "ask first" policy is helpful in conversations with friends about their problems. If we go into the conversation with a commitment to asking the person a question like, "How are you?" or "How can I help?" our advice will be better informed. We may even discover that our advice isn't what our friend needs at all. This is also good advice for men conversing with women about their experiences of harassment, or white people engaging people of color about their experiences of racism. Make it your policy to ask questions first, listen carefully, caring about the others' experiences, and offer your own thoughts later, if at all. And if it's a new policy for you, have the questions prepared ("How can I help?") so you don't fall back on old habits ("Here's what you should do.").

The advantage of a pre-commitment to a "once a day" or "once per conversation" policy is that it doesn't rely on our ability to see when humility is needed (an ability we may not yet have). Such policies allow us to fake it 'til we make it. Or, as Aristotle would have put it, you can eventually develop a better character by behaving in a more virtuous fashion. We can use these strategies to develop *habits* of humility, which we hope will eventually become second nature.

The key to humility in our relationships, then, is that we shouldn't think we know everything, and we should be willing to admit that and take steps to improve.

This description of the humble person makes humility challenging, but still in our reach. Cultivating humility means cultivating a practice of acting and thinking in a certain way— with perspective on the importance of our own viewpoint in the cosmos, mindful of our limits, and open to the experiences of others. We'll fail sometimes, and it's important to fail so that we can correct and adjust in our next action, our next opportunity. The good news about cultivating humility is that you don't have to be perfect at it! With humility, acknowledging the need for it is half the battle.

in the foreground and background

JOURNALISM IN AN ERA OF LIKES, FOLLOWS, AND SHARES

Lynette Clemetson

I got my start in print journalism in the 1990s. And like most journalists who came up before the dominance of the internet and of social media, I was taught that I was not supposed to be part of the story. Be a tough questioner, sure. But perhaps more importantly, be a good listener, an astute observer, able to maintain enough distance to take clear-eyed stock of a person, event, or unfolding situation.

My first real lessons of humility and reporting were at *Newsweek* magazine, when I was freelancing in Hong Kong in the years leading up to Hong Kong's handover from Britain to Chinese rule in 1997. In my twenties and full of ambition, I was itching to write cover stories and see my byline in bold print in the front of the magazine. The Asia editor, Steven Strasser, was based in Hong Kong, a luxury of a bygone era when foreign bureaus abounded and regional media hubs buzzed with the competitive energy of multiple international magazines, newspapers, and broadcast networks.

Newsweek's Hong Kong bureau, a glass-encased jewel on the forty-seventh floor of the Bank of China Tower overlooking Victoria Harbour, glistened before me with all that was possible in an adventurous international journalism career. As I sat wide-eyed in front of Steve's desk, he generously fielded my big pitches, and gently slowed me down.

"Never use a quote for something you can say better in your own words, and never let your own words smother something you can say better with a quote," Steve guided me, as he marked up and handed back my early copy. "When you can write one column [of a magazine page], then I'll let you write two. When you can write two columns, then a page. Remember not to get in the way of your story." And so it went.

"Remember not to get in the way of your story." I wasn't conscious of it at the time, but those early primers on form, structure, and pacing were teaching me to approach and infuse my journalism with a sense of humility. To some, the words journalism and humility might seem incongruous. Holding the powerful to account suggests a certain brashness. Yet humility is a cornerstone of reporting, an essential starting point in the pursuit of truth.

Take a look in a dictionary or thesaurus. Many of the words associated with humility are antithetical to the bold aims of journalism: lowliness, submissiveness, docility, timidity, diffidence, subservience. These synonyms align more with preserving the status quo than questioning it.

But alongside the more servile associations, there is one synonym for humility in some dictionaries that fits well within a journalistic context: unobtrusiveness. Unobtrusiveness—not getting in the way— is an aspect of humility that is critical for reporters, whose job it is to document, interpret, and analyze the world around them.

Because journalists are tasked with digging and asking difficult questions, it can be easy to think of journalism as primarily intrusive. But pursuing clarity, stepping back and approaching an issue with a broad set of questions, requires a kind of unobtrusive humility, a belief that understanding something or someone requires patience, curiosity, and often repeated and varied approaches.

An unobtrusive posture and approach toward reporting can be hard to maintain in a media landscape defined by branding, influencers, and talking heads. The need for self-promotion to reach key audiences across multiple platforms creates a difficult balancing act for reporters, whose work relies to a considerable extent on the ability to recede into the background, to be astute observers, questioners, trackers, and listeners. The pace and pressure in journalism today can leave reporters one impulsive Tweet away from a loss of credibility on a daily basis.

This is not some wistful ode to the past. I am not someone who is overly nostalgic about the good ol' days of journalism, or anything else. I have changed my habits in step with the industry. I use social media daily, both to consume information and to share it. For the past decade I have worked with reporters on expanding the reach of journalism and building their careers in this complex new information system we now inhabit. I extoll the many professional benefits of the digital worlds we now all hold in our hands. Information is easier to find, easier to check. Data is easier to access and sort. Disruption of the journalism industry has cracked open the old system of media gatekeepers ostensibly allowing for greater diversity and representation of voices and experiences.

Many reporters navigate today's information terrain brilliantly, with savvy and seeming ease. Nikole Hannah-Jones of *The New York Times* has transformed the national conversation on systemic racism by taking a deeply personal approach to her reporting on pervasive issues facing African

Americans. She engages in a running social media conversation with her followers and detractors on the subjects she writes about. From her coverage on inequities in education to her sweeping 1619 Project, which reframed our understanding of America's founding history, her reporting has been socially relevant precisely because she has used new platforms to her advantage and challenged journalistic conventions long enforced under the questionable guise of objectivity.

The Washington Post's David Fahrenthold brought greater transparency to the work of political reporting when, in 2017, he posted pictures of his notebook on Twitter and enlisted his then hundreds of thousands of followers in helping him track down leads in his investigation of Donald Trump's charitable giving.

Used smartly, the digital and social tools journalists now have at their disposal can bolster their credibility, deepen their storytelling, and reinforce their humanity.

But it is also true that hot takes and hive feedback can complicate decision-making and obscure the desire of most reporters to simply let their work speak for itself. It can get in the way.

Ta-Nehisi Coates perhaps framed the tension most succinctly when he deleted his Twitter account in 2017 after a high-profile feud on the platform with scholar Cornel West: "peace ya'll. i'm out. I didn't get in it for this," Coates told his then-1.25 million followers.

Many years ago, Gwen Ifill, Michele Norris, and Michel Martin made notable moves to public media, each demonstrating how to bring their full identities and priorities to the public media culture. No one would have dared call any of these women "docile" or any of the submissive stand-ins for humility. But unobtrusive, yes. I would argue that that definition of humility held up for each of them. With their own distinct styles, in their story choices, questioning, and listening, they each brought to their broadcast work a deep understanding of and respect for the space they inhabited and they used their platforms to surface the voices, experiences, and stories of people who might not otherwise be included in our conversations or consciousness. The way they created a sense of intimacy, of being seen and heard, in public media informed how I moved into the space after honing my craft as a print journalist.

A few years after I had been in Washington D.C., years before I went to NPR, I sought Gwen's advice as I was weighing competing job offers to leave *Newsweek*. "Which place scares you the most?" she asked me. We got our hair done at the same place, often at the same time with different stylists, and I always knew where to find her when I needed an ear. "The place that scares you most is probably the place where you'll do your best work," she argued, because it would propel me to prove to everybody, and myself, that I belonged. But she added a caveat. "Just remember at each place you work to hold onto yourself and what you value."

"Hold on to what you value." I wrote that nugget down in the notebook I always carried with me. Like Steve's lessons, I think Gwen's advice was telling me to keep a sense of humility at the center of my work, and not allow the seeming glamor of a big journalism job to pull me off-center and away from the searching curiosity that led me to the field.

Taking that advice, I went to *The New York Times*, and was lucky to sit near Robin Toner, the first woman to become national political correspondent for the paper. Robin was nobody's pushover. But she was one of the most humble and hardworking journalists I have ever met. On any given evening I could see Robin running through the meticulous fact-checking system that she applied to every single story she wrote. With more than 1,900 bylines in her career at the *Times*, she only had six printed corrections.

In the midst of her intense work routine, Robin would always answer any question I had on some facet of politics or policy that I was trying to weave into a story. And she did it all while taking afterschool calls from her young twins, never trying to hide the fact that she had a full and chaotic life and that balancing it all was no easy task. "It's always the small mistakes that will come back to bite you," she said. So she checked and checked and checked every detail in every story. I was never as good at it as Robin was. No one was. But I wrote it down in my personal notebook. "Check the small details."

"Don't get in the way of your story."

"Hold on to what you value."

"Check the small details."

These simple bits of wisdom are the kind of guideposts that don't change, no matter how platforms or trends shift. And if the unglamorous humility of the work doesn't come naturally, a reporting career will teach it to you in unexpected moments it over time.

Some of the most uncomfortable lessons on humility come when you are forced to navigate someone else's space and lived experience, moments when you have to wrestle with pulling back and waiting, observing a humble, unobtrusive posture, sometimes in excruciatingly intrusive encounters. In May 1999, after the Columbine mass school shooting. I was assigned, as part of *Newsweek*'s national reporting team on the ground, to cover the victim's families. Part of my job was to try to get non-yearbook pictures of the children who were killed. To do that, you have to introduce yourself to grieving parents and ask them for pictures of their child who has just been murdered.

As I talked to one family, sitting in their living room, on their couch, the parents were being very open with me—a stranger, a reporter, who was one among hundreds descending on their town in the midst of unthinkable tragedy. I asked for a picture of their son and they brought one. He was much younger in the picture, so I asked if they had one that was more recent. The mother was holding a shoebox full of pictures, and I could see something cross her face. Suddenly I was in the middle of a deeply personal moment as I watched a woman realize she couldn't find many pictures she had taken of her son in the past year.

Her expression went nearly blank as she shuffled through the pictures in the box. It was an excruciatingly uncomfortable moment and I wanted desperately to be anywhere else. I did my best to disappear in plain sight, to sit silently and recede until she was ready to acknowledge my presence again. She finally did, with surprising kindness, and we settled on a picture for the magazine. I did not write the shoebox moment into my reporting. But it informed my understanding of the many painful personal moments obscured in the midst of the most public tragedies. And I keep the feeling of that moment with me as I have encountered similar moments in reporting and editing since then.

Most journalists have these moments throughout their career that shape and inform the care that they bring to their work. Journalists building their careers today, under pressure for immediacy and incremental updates, have to work harder to navigate the space between what to observe for understanding and what to share, what to respond to and push out in real time and what to hold back, out of respect or for the sake of the story.

If fact, I think that even as journalists learn to smartly build public sharing into their work, most people drawn to reporting as a way to make a living yearn for time away from social media and public platforms and the expectation of constant engagement. Most journalists are drawn to digging, thinking, and asking questions, not to sharing their own thoughts and being out front.

⌒⌒⌒

Over the past decade, I've been in leadership roles in newsrooms, editing and developing the careers of young reporters, hopefully with the same intention and care that was given to me by my own mentors and editors. And for the past several years I've been in the privileged role of leading a journalism fellowship at the University of Michigan. The Knight-Wallace Fellowship offers accomplished journalists one academic year, working closely within a cohort of other journalists, to sharpen their skills and push themselves in new directions.

Each year I read hundreds of applications from journalists eager for an opportunity to step back from their harried pace and take stock of how they are approaching their craft. Regardless of the profile of the applicant—whether they practice journalism through text, audio, or visual storytelling, whether they focus on daily news or longform magazine writing—there is one common thread that runs through nearly all of the applications. They all express a desire for the rare gift of time, the desire to approach their work more intentionally, to step back and reconnect with what they got into it for in the first place.

The very act of applying is a demonstration of humility. Think about it, just when your career has hit a good enough stride that someone would think of you as "accomplished," to throw up your hand and say, "You know, I think I need to step out for a minute and re-evaluate how I am doing things." Every year the process is a brand new miracle to me.

I know what it takes to fill out and submit the application, because I was a Knight-Wallace Fellow myself in 2009, several years before I became director of the program. Having built my career as a print reporter, I had taken a turn toward digital strategy and management, and I wasn't sure I had made the right call. I wasn't sure whether I was making the kind of choices Gwen Ifill had counseled me about years earlier or whether I was just running for survival in a rapidly changing industry. The fellowship helped me reconnect with my skills and motivations, helped me remember the bits of wisdom I had written in my little notebook years before. By the time the fellowship year ended, I was ready to step back into management with the kind of enthusiasm, intention and, I think, humility that I had developed working as a reporter.

Each September now, when a new class of fellows starts, one of the first things I tell them is to put away their phones. While we're engaged in our seminars, they're not allowed to Tweet and, typically, for the first couple of months I don't really expect them to be producing ANYTHING. Their job is to observe, and listen—to our speakers, to one another, to themselves—and to try to figure out where the experience is pointing them.

For most of the fellows—hard-running journalists, mostly in their 30s and 40s—this directive is a little nerve-wracking. For some, it's downright destabilizing. But for nearly everyone it provides some sense of relief. And nearly all fellows leave the program better journalists, more connected to the curiosity and humility that drew them to the field.

Docile, lowly, timid, subservient. I'd never hang those monikers on the journalists I know. But if humility is an expressed interest in how things work and why, a sincere curiosity about the differences and complexities of people's realities, experiences, motives, and challenges, and a yearning to understand those complexities and explain them to others, well that's the humility in journalism that I was drawn to and taught to develop. And I think that's what drives most journalists I know, regardless of their follows, likes, and shares.

TEXTUAL STEALING?
COPYRIGHT, RACE, AND
ELUSIVE JUSTICE

Gilbert B. Rodman

t's hard for me to feel much sympathy for Robin Thicke.
He's a white man who's garnered a lot of fame and fortune
for himself making Black music, and he's done so without
showing the sort of humility that typically separates respectful
borrowing from cultural appropriation. To be clear, such
humility is not something that can be measured using some
simple objective formula, and cases that might seem to be
"obvious" examples of "good" borrowing to some observers
are ones where reasonable people can (and often do) disagree.
That said, it's relatively easy to recognize cases where such
humility is missing—and Thicke's is among this latter group.

His story is not that of a poor white boy who fell in
love with Black music, and then honed his craft in obscurity
until his big break came along (cf. Elvis Presley). Nor is he a
fan from outside a creative community who found a willing
mentor on the inside to nurture his talent and help establish his
credibility within the tradition (cf. Eminem). Instead, Thicke
is a dude—in all the less-than-noble senses of that term—born
into a show business family, and whose career benefited from
the name recognition and industry connections that were his
birthright. To be fair, he's not an opportunistic hack in the
same way that Pat Boone or Vanilla Ice were, but he's still

much closer to the Boone/Ice end of the spectrum than he is to the Elvis/Eminem end.

Identifying where any given musician belongs on that spectrum is admittedly more of an art than a science, and any semi-comprehensive attempt to explain that art would take more space than is available here. But one of the most important things to look/listen for is whether a white musician working within a Black genre treats the music as an aesthetic tradition that deserves respect and care, or as a gimmicky thing that can be exploited and/or mocked. Boone, for example, made it clear that he didn't particularly like R&B, and he only covered songs originally performed by artists such as Little Richard and Fats Domino because there was a market for "respectable" white versions of R&B hits that he could profit from. Vanilla Ice was less openly cynical about his foray into hip-hop, but to anyone who had been paying serious attention to the genre, his music sounded more like a weak novelty act than a serious attempt to find a respectable place for himself within the tradition. Elvis and Eminem, on the other hand, both made serious efforts to acknowledge and honor the Black musicians who had come before them—and did so even at early stages of their careers, when it would arguably have been more profitable for them to distance themselves from the Blackness of the music they were making. Thicke appears to have more respect for Black musical traditions than Boone or Ice ever did but, in sharp contrast to Elvis or Eminem, he also presents himself as if his right to claim a piece of that tradition for himself is self-evident, rather than something that he needs to earn with humility and hard work.

The history of popular music is filled with tales of white folks stealing Black music and being amply rewarded for that theft, and so it would be easy to see Thicke's legal setbacks as a kind of righteous justice for more than a century of cultural appropriation that's largely gone unpunished . . . but that would be the wrong conclusion to reach, since the 2015 court verdict against Thicke (and his "co-"songwriter, Pharrell Williams) for copyright infringement—which was upheld on final appeal in December 2018—is a travesty. As unsympathetic a character as he may be, Thicke deserves better. So does Williams. More importantly, so do the rest of us.

The case in question revolved around Thicke's 2013 hit single "Blurred Lines," which a California jury found to be too similar to Motown legend Marvin Gaye's 1977 hit "Got to Give It Up." It's a confounding and problematic verdict in many ways. Unless one is so unfamiliar with R&B as to think that it all sounds the same, it's hard to confuse "Lines" with "Got." This is not a "U Can't Touch This"/"Super Freak" kind of case, where the main hook that drives both songs is identical, and you need to hear the vocals to be sure which one you're listening to. Nor is this a "He's So Fine"/"My Sweet Lord" type of case, where the melodies are so similar that you can sing the lyrics of either one over the other and never miss a beat. If "Lines" infringes on "Got," it does so in a way that's so subtle (or so trivial) that it defies reasonable understandings of what "infringement" actually involves. More crucially, it opens the door for any new text that "feels" like some prior text to be declared "guilty" of infringement—and there aren't many (if any) texts that can lay claim to the sort of untainted originality that such a standard would create.

In spite of the formal claims about infringement that the Gaye family needed to make in order to get this case into the courts in the first place, what's *really* at stake in the battle over "Lines" is the aforementioned ugly history of cultural appropriation: i.e., white folks who took Black music, claimed it as their own, and got rich and famous in the process, even though the white versions of that music were often aesthetically weak imitations of the originals. Meanwhile, an awful lot of Black artists with much more talent than their imitators wound up languishing in (relative) poverty and obscurity, and huge swaths of Black cultural and aesthetic history have been marginalized or erased in favor of whitewashed versions of the story. This is the story of what (white) minstrelsy did to (Black) field songs, what swing did to jazz, what rock 'n' roll did to rhythm 'n' blues, and so on.

Thicke is an obvious target for an attempt at this sort of restorative justice for at least three reasons:

Reason #1. Talent is a tricky (if not impossible) thing to measure in a clean, objective fashion—tastes vary, after all—but Thicke is still clearly much less talented than Gaye. He doesn't have Gaye's broad aesthetic vision. He doesn't have Gaye's multi-instrumental fluency. He doesn't have anything close to Gaye's singing voice. And if you want to find a textbook example of cultural appropriation, it's mediocre white dudes who manage to achieve superstar-level success while working in a Black idiom. As the best-selling single in the world in 2013, "Blurred Lines" fits this description without trying very hard. I can't say it doesn't have a catchy groove—it does—but none of that is thanks to Thicke. Which leads to:

Reason #2. I should amend a part of what I just wrote. If there's *really* a textbook example of cultural appropriation, it's white dudes claiming authorship—in whole or in part—for songs that were actually written entirely by Black folks. And Thicke did that here too. As the infringement trial made clear, the real (and sole) songwriter for "Lines" was Pharrell Williams (who is Black). But Thicke wound up with partial credit anyway, thanks to a very old, very common, very shady practice in the music business. The scam in question here doesn't work exclusively across racial lines—a lot of "green" songwriters (Black, white, and otherwise) have been forced to share songwriting credit (and thus royalties) with producers, managers, record company execs, and even deejays—but this is still one of the major ways that Black songwriters have been ripped off for decades. And while Gaye's heirs weren't suing Thicke to help Williams recover royalties that, arguably, should have belonged entirely to him all along (and, to be fair, Williams wasn't an entirely unwitting victim here), the fact that Thicke was legally entitled to *any* royalties for a song that he didn't write at all adds his name to a very long list of white folks who've gotten credit (and money) for creative work done by Black artists.

Reason #3. The public controversy over "Lines" and its "rapey" lyrics had no direct bearing on the questions that were before the jury in the infringement case. But it *did* render Thicke a less-than-sympathetic public figure which, in turn, made him a particularly juicy target for a lawsuit. (There's more than a little irony here. Gaye may be a much-beloved member of the soul/R&B pantheon, but his personal sexual politics were far from ideal and, in ways that should be clear from the title alone, "Give" isn't exactly a sensitive expression of tender romance or pressure-free desire.) Still, the Gaye family was fighting this case in the court of public opinion as much as (if not more than) they were in a court of law. So it didn't hurt the symbolic side of their efforts that they were aiming to punish a much-maligned "bad boy" celebrity, rather than a beloved white crossover figure such as Adele or Dusty Springfield.

In spite of how deserving a target Thicke might seem to be, however, and though it brings me no pleasure to take his side over Gaye's (even in part), I still want to argue that the Gaye family's suit was a misguided effort to achieve any real sense of restorative justice. When we talk about cultural appropriation, after all, we're talking about something more than just theft at the level of individual artists. We're talking about an institutionally sanctioned kind of cultural and economic theft that is supported by a hierarchical, racialized system of legal, economic, and political power. It's those practices and that system that turn culture into private property in the first place. It's those practices and that system that make it hard (if not impossible) for people of color on the "wrong" end of that system to fight back against appropriation. And, to the extent that a handful of people of color *do* get their day in court, the best that they can ever hope for is a decision limited to a very specific (and, in the big picture, a very tiny) instance of appropriation, while the larger, everyday practices of institutionalized theft continue unchecked. Copyright law doesn't have any provisions for the type of justice that's really at issue here, since it's rooted in the assumption that culture is comprised of discrete, individual texts, each of which is the property of discrete, individual creators. There's no room here for collective ownership or communal property rights, and no obvious way to address injustice on a structural, systemic level.

As such, even if we were to accept that "Lines" infringes on "Got" (and that claim still strikes me as a stretch), Thicke is *not* the real villain in this story. To be sure, he benefits here in ways that he shouldn't have. But he's not much more than a pawn in the industry's larger game. Maybe, given his star status, he's a knight. But he's definitely not the king or queen. He is, at best, a convenient scapegoat: a symbolic trophy, but not the sort of major power broker whose punishment might actually affect industry-level practices of appropriation and exploitation.

On the opposite side of this case, we should also recognize that, if the goal is some sort of restorative justice around cultural appropriation, then neither Gaye nor his family are anywhere near the top of the list of deserving recipients of that sort of financial windfall. To be clear, I suspect that Gaye was exploited and cheated by industry suits over the course of his career— probably more than once—and his fame and fortune would probably have been even greater than they were if (somehow) he had been a white man with comparable musical talent and genius. But the multi-million dollar court-mandated payout from Thicke and Williams to Gaye's heirs won't do anything to end—or even slow down—cultural appropriation. It won't stop labels from promoting white R&B artists more heavily and broadly than they do Black ones. It won't stop white industry bigwigs from stealing songwriting credits from Black musicians. It won't stop white audiences from embracing Black music made by white artists more readily and eagerly than they embrace Black artists. It won't stop white folks from fetishizing "authentic" Black music in ways that still marginalize it and distort its history. It won't help to put money in the pockets of Black musical pioneers who never got the fame or fortune they deserved.

Most problematically, though, now that the final legal appeals are over, the "Blurred Lines" case presents a much larger threat to restorative justice for cultural appropriation than would have existed had the Gaye family lost. A large part of what originally got Thicke and Williams in trouble was that they openly acknowledged that they admired Gaye's music and had aimed to create new music reflecting that influence. (It didn't help matters that this gesture in Gaye's direction felt more arrogant than humble, more boastful than respectful.) Given that the connection between "Lines" and "Got" is *not* obvious unless someone works hard to "reveal" the similarities between the two songs, this case might never have happened at all if Thicke and Williams had simply claimed that they came up with the beat entirely on their own.

If Thicke is an unsympathetic character (in part) because he never displayed the kind of humility that we would ideally like to see from white folks working in Black idioms, then one of the major ironies of the verdict against him is that it's likely to *discourage* future artists from being humble and respectful enough to acknowledge their influences. It's bad enough that the "Blurred Lines" case threatens to stifle the creativity of artists whose work "feels" like older work without actually copying it. But there's no real justice to be found in a case where one of the major lessons it offers to future artists is to hide and/or deny their influences. If we truly want people to be humble enough to recognize and honor the giants on whose shoulders they are standing, then we also need to create and maintain a culture around creative work where such acknowledgments are encouraged and welcomed, rather than punished.

IN-BETWEEN SPACES

Ami Walsh

While a hospital room is not an optimal sound studio—it may not be possible to silence beeping machines, hisses from oxygen tubes, voices from the other side of the curtain or out in the hall—it is a private and even sacred space, one that seems to give people the inspiration and courage to say things that they may never have said in quite the same way before.

The oldest patient I have worked with was a woman in her late eighties. Her daughter and granddaughter had been in the room when she told the story of meeting her husband on an Easter morning in 1948 (they were together fifty-five years, raising six children). She described the small town in Tennessee where they first met and how he courted her by writing letters. "Back then," she said, "the only way we had of writing letters was to put pennies in the mailbox with the letter to send it off."

As often happens with other patients, the moment the recorder was turned on, she seemed to fall into a kind of storytelling trance, getting lost in the details and finding details she had lost: the white cake and chocolate syrup she'd had on her wedding night, the biscuits and fried chicken, the wishbone she discovered when she pulled apart the breast meat. When she finished, her daughter expressed surprise at the energy her mother had mustered, the vivid details she'd recovered. Her daughter asked if this was something that happened with other patients or whether it was a sign her mother had a special gift.

One evening a week I meet with patients at University Hospital, the main care center at Michigan Medicine in Ann Arbor, and help them to record personal narratives. When I started doing this eight years ago, I had no idea if people would want to—or be feeling well enough—to record stories. Neither did my colleagues at Michigan Medicine, who offered to train me to work in the hospital as part of a bedside arts program called Gifts of Art and provide supervision. Hospital-based narrative art programs traditionally focus on offering patients writing opportunities. Giving patients the chance to record a story in their hospital rooms was something entirely new.

I was inspired to try because for several years I'd had success recording stories with pediatric patients in a non-hospital setting. The children attended a weeklong summer camp run by the University of Michigan Transplant Center. Many had developmental delays and ADHD due to their chronic illnesses. Some had trouble holding a pencil because their hands shook from their immunosuppressant medications. We focused on creating a safe and playful space for kids to make, share, and listen to stories. The recorder allowed every child to become a published storyteller in the brief span of a forty-minute workshop. While our activity wasn't as popular with campers as the climbing wall or archery, it had an enthusiastic following and continues to thrive today.

The most remarkable stories often come from children who seem least likely to say anything at all: the homesick girl who will not look anyone in the eye or the boy who will not stop drumming his pencil on the table. The kids seem as surprised as anyone to hear their voices coming out of the speakers telling beautiful stories about everything from fairies to ghosts, ziplining to new friends.

When I arrived for my first shift at the hospital, I hoped something similar might happen with the adults I was about to visit. I had a list of referrals from hospital staff but the first several patients weren't interested. Aside from taking too long to explain the program, I kept mentioning "work," as in we could "work together to create a story or poem." I had used poems and imaginative exercises to help the kids get started on a story, but these patients weren't interested in prompts.

By the time I introduced myself to a woman in a single room on the sixth floor, I simply asked if she had a story that she'd like to record to give to someone special in her life. She thought for a moment then said, "Do I have stories? I have so many stories."

She invited me to take a seat next to her bed. When the recorder was turned on, she began: "Once upon a time." Without a moment's hesitation, she told a fictional story about a teddy bear named Tommy. I later learned she'd been writing a series of children's stories about this teddy bear, a childhood gift from her grandfather during her first hospitalization, after a car accident many years ago.

While I was playing back her piece, a group of University of Michigan athletes came into her room. As part of a volunteer program called "Michigan from the Heart," student-athletes visit patients in the hospital one evening a week. Here they were, seven or eight young men and women dressed in maize and blue, crowded into her room. The patient wanted them to hear her story. "I want the world to hear it," is what she told us.

When the recording ended, the small room erupted with the athletes' cheers. Later, I heard her say, "I've been waiting for this my whole life."

Week after week, I began to meet with patients who—now that I had re-framed the activity as a "gift"—wanted to record a story. The invitation for people to express themselves and to create a story for someone they loved seemed to motivate even those who initially didn't think they had anything to say. Or those who might not have known where to begin.

But once patients imagine a listener who matters, what they want to say often comes effortlessly into focus. Suddenly there's an intention to share something meaningful with another person, and to create something new. If they aren't sure how to organize their story, I often suggest a simple structure with a beginning, middle, and end. If linear time doesn't make sense as an organizing principle, I may propose a list poem, a letter, or even a song. I invite them to assume an active role in shaping and arranging their material. The sense of structure gives them confidence in the process. They may not know exactly what they are going to say when the recorder is turned on, but they now have enough confidence in the narrative possibilities—and in their abilities—to start recording.

When they trust me as their guide, I feel a kind of humility flourishing between us. Neither of us is certain how the recording will turn out, but we have a belief in the potential of each another, and in the potential of our collaboration. A door opens, and we walk through it.

We are not alone. The presence of an audience, seen and unseen, brings many listeners into the room and gives the recording session a palpable charge. Patients are at once performing for an intimate known audience (their selected listeners), a relative stranger (me), as well as other implied potential audiences. There is an awareness that the digital file can be broadcast on any channel, social or otherwise. Most participants choose to keep their stories private. But some have published their pieces on Facebook and YouTube or over sound systems as part of a community event or family gathering. One man recorded his own eulogy, which he intended to broadcast at his funeral.

One patient, who made a nearly hour-long autobiographical recording about her life, described her experience this way: "These thoughts have been swirling around for so long in here," she said, touching her head. "And also"—she tapped a spot above her heart—"in here…I feel a sense of relief having gotten my story out to someone other than someone in my family—having gotten it out, period. I think that if I had stood before my family to give it to them, they would think, 'Oh, we've heard it before.'"

Most patients tell far shorter stories—ten to twenty minutes on average. They seem to know precisely how to compress what they want to say to match the amount of energy they have to give toward the telling. I can often feel an ending approaching before it arrives. The room seems to go suddenly silent after they say their last word. I often feel that they, like me, want to stay a moment longer in the place their story has transported us to.

Here's another remarkable thing about these recordings: They come out fully shaped and with tremendous emotion, as if propelled by the kind of life force choreographer and dancer Martha Graham famously talked about when she spoke about creativity. "There is a vitality, a life force, a quickening that is translated through you into action," she said, "and because there is only one of you in all time, this expression is unique. And if you block it, it will never exist through any other medium and be lost. The world will not have it. It is not your business to determine how good it is, nor how valuable it is, nor how it compares with other expressions. It is your business to keep it yours clearly and directly, to keep the channel open."

A willingness to keep the channel open: This gets close to defining what humility means to me. I don't think of it as a thing that anyone can definitively possess; rather it is a willingness to step into uncertainty despite the emotional risks. This willingness sets something unique about you in motion—a life, a story, a breath—moving toward a place it's never been before. It's the kind of humility I've been privileged to witness in my role helping people to record deeply moving personal stories.

That first year, as the weeks passed, the colleagues who provided oversight of my work with patients at the hospital (Dr. Jeffrey Evans, a rehabilitation psychology and neuropsychology clinician, and Gifts of Art Director Elaine Sims) began to wonder how the storytelling experience might benefit hospitalized patients. A research project was launched, which marked a small but significant change in my interactions with patients: At the end of our time together, I asked each if they would be willing to share their audio recording for educational purposes and participate in two follow-up interviews. Fifty-five patients agreed. Five of our patients and their families granted permission to have excerpts from their audio stories featured in that publication.

I encourage you to visit the website where the paper was published (bit.ly/JHR_storystudio) to hear them for yourself.

Until then, we hadn't asked patients to share their stories with anyone outside our team. Initially the main reason was patient privacy—all files are confidential and shared only with expressed written consent. Promotional posting, especially on social media, contradicts the mission of our program, which is to "honor the patient's sense of self, offer comfort and hope, and to support a hospital experience that dignifies the individual." A good measure of that dignity comes from giving patients control over what they want to say, how they want to say it, and how and where they want to share it.

Listening to the audio recordings is really the only way to appreciate them. Transcribing the words on the page diminishes the fullness of their expression. It's not the words but the in-between sounds—the pacing, inflections, utterances, and pauses—that give them their expressive intensity.

One of my writing teachers, Kevin McIlvoy, has devoted himself for years to the study of the human voice so that he might, as he says, "*feel* my way into being a better listener." This experience of becoming a better listener is precisely what I feel when I am helping to facilitate a storytelling session. When I hear the longing for connection in people's voices, I become far more attentive and present than I am in my everyday life. I've also witnessed this change in others. The first time was that night in 2012, when I stood inside a patient's hospital room with a group of college athletes. I've witnessed it many times since then, as the recordings have been shared with students, clinical staff, and arts and healthcare professionals at conferences.

Listening becomes a powerful shared experience that seems to open listeners to their own feelings of vulnerability and longing for connection. Most strikingly, this happened during a mini-course with second-year students at the University of Michigan Medical School. After playing a selection of patient audio stories, the students made their own recordings. They took emotional risks. They shared intimate experiences. They were surprised by what they created. Afterwards, one student wrote, "Hearing the other students' stories and the stories you have recorded in the hospital leaves me fulfilled in a way that I haven't felt since starting medical school."

Our observations and own experiences have raised compelling questions about the value of community listening events. How does listening in the presence of others differ from listening when we're alone and plugged into devices? What might we discover about human connectedness and our capacity—both individual and collective—to become better listeners if we're more intentional about creating respectful spaces that honor both storytellers and listeners?

From our small sample size, we have seen that playing just one or two expressive recordings consistently inspires listeners to share their own meaningful stories about life challenges and triumphs, sorrows and joys.

Our task now is to keep the channel open.

even in moments of humiliation

THE LOSER'S GUIDE TO WINNING: NEW DEFINITIONS OF SUCCESS FROM SPORT'S GREATEST FAILURES

Mickey Duzyj

In 2019, I created a documentary series called *Losers* for Netflix. The show reconnected with eight of the sporting world's most infamous failures—golf's Jean Van De Velde, figure skating's Surya Bonaly, and boxing's Michael Bentt, to name a few—asking if time had changed how they felt about their misfortune. More than anything, I wanted to know: if we learn more from our failures than we do from our successes, what lessons can we learn from those who have lost?

Some of what I learned was unsurprising. The athletes by and large felt cold cruelty from their fans and their peers; branded as "losers", they were forced from the stage by a media culture that reveres winning. But there was also a curveball: across the board, these professional athletes—as self-directed as exist in any profession—came away from their public failures on a similar trajectory, moving away from self-centeredness and toward altruistic connections with causes larger than themselves. The transformations they experienced were dramatic and fulfilling, turning the group of notorious "losers" into clear winners in life. Spending time with them forced me to confront whether our culture's definitions of "winning" and "success" could use an upgrade. It's a lesson that's especially relevant during a time when a pandemic, creeping authoritarianism, and acts of racism have left many of us with an acute sense of loss.

In a widely-circulated clip from the docuseries *The Last Dance*, renowned winner Michael Jordan dismisses criticism of his notorious brutality—including punching a teammate in the face—as coming from "people who haven't won anything." (Read: they're losers.) If you overheard your boss say this, you might react with horror. But decades after Jordan was first held up as a role model for young people, through Nike's "Be Like Mike" campaign and beyond, an unspoken message seems clear: winning *should* matter more than anything, and if you win, the ends will justify the means, no matter how ruthless those means are.

Few would fault Jordan for his ambition, but there is a dark side to a culture defining individual achievement as the pinnacle of success. The flipside of associating virtue with those who are rich, famous, and victorious (a construct that's problematic enough,) is that we simultaneously condemn the character of those who *haven't* achieved, who haven't made the cut. You need only skim the daily news headlines to see the consequences of this mentality: leadership's shrug about mass unemployment, an epidemic of trolling, and a class of "winners" freely exploiting those with less social standing. To be a "loser" in 2020 is to have a target on your back.

Many of the athletes I profiled spent their early lives following our culture's blueprint of success, connecting their value as individuals to their personal performance in competition. When they met with failure—often before large crowds of onlookers—their disappointment came with a permanent loss of reputation.

As their losses came to define their careers, the athletes began to see the pitfalls of defining success only through their personal performance. Looking outside themselves, they found new empathy for others similarly dismissed as "losers," and considered new ways to define success in their lives.

Jean Van De Velde, a French golfer lampooned for his meltdown during the 1999 Open Championship, overcame his failure when he realized that his infamy could be put to charitable ends. These days, he's much prouder of his legacy as a Unicef ambassador—raising hundreds of thousands of dollars for impoverished children—than he is of his long golf career. And he couldn't be less bothered by his position atop every "Great Collapses in Sporting History" listicle.

Surya Bonaly, a Black figure skater, had a career defined by the harsh, racist judges of her overwhelmingly white sport. The judges regarded her unique abilities and approach as inartistic. She narrowly missed winning Olympic medals on multiple occasions and became a pariah after protesting her second place finish at the 1994 World Championships. Now retired from competition, Surya spends her time coaching and mentoring young athletes of color. While she urges them to strive for excellence—as athletes, students, and citizens—she's also quick to remind them that medals aren't everything. As Bonaly says, this obsession "can destroy you."

Basketball player "Blackjack" Ryan saw his defiant, self-sabotaging streak get him kicked off a series of college teams, undermining a career that could have earned him millions in the pros. Today, he's a member of the Harlem Wizards, performing tricks and sharing motivational messages to audiences around the country. When asked if he regrets his missed opportunities, Ryan told me that his current work is his true calling, bringing him more self-esteem and satisfaction than anything in his professional past.

Arthur Miller wrote that "possibly the greatest truths we know come out of people's suffering." In the year I observed the subjects of *Losers,* the truth they gained seemed crystal clear: true success has less to do with individual achievement and more to do with selflessly giving to others.

Reimagining a culture with healthier definitions of success means dismantling the myth that "winning" is only defined through personal achievement. In a loss-filled year like 2020, where many of us were forced to consider new definitions of success in our own lives, it should be relieving to know that there are those who have survived loss in admirable ways, giving us all new blueprints to find success in our lives.

We can start by aspiring to be less like Michael Jordan and more like Jean Van De Velde.

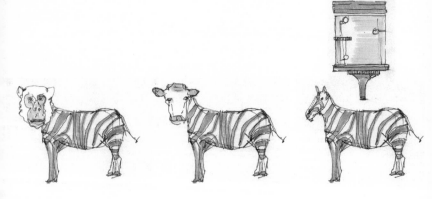

EPIC FAILURES IN 3D PRINTING

Nadia Danienta and Aric Rindfleisch

If you're reading this essay, you're reading it in a book or device that you did not make. Most of us are far removed from the making process. Since the dawn of the Industrial Revolution, the tools used to make the things we want and need have become increasingly centralized and controlled by companies. Thus, most of the things we own have been made by someone we don't know, in a place we've never been, using tools we've never seen.

In contrast to the Industrial Revolution's centralization of production, the emerging digital revolution is highly decentralized and has made the tools of creation—desktop computers, video cameras, editing software—widely accessible and quite affordable. To date, these tools have mainly digitized forms of communication such as music, text, and video. The recent emergence of accessible and affordable desktop 3D printers represents a different direction by providing a growing number of individuals with the ability to create a variety of physical products ranging from phone cases to prosthetics. For example, Arielle Rausin, a former member of the University of Illinois' Wheelchair Racing Team used desktop 3D printing technology to make her own customized wheelchair racing gloves.

**Arielle Rausin's 3D printed
wheelchair racing gloves.**
Photo credit: MakerLab at UIUC.

While the act of making often generates a sense of pride, it can also be quite humbling. Things rarely go as planned and our creations often don't live up to our imagination. The risk of failure is especially high when employing desktop 3D printers, as this tool is still at an early stage of development and most people have little, if any, formal training. For most of us, making an object via a 3D printer is not an easy task. The difficulty of using this technology has led a prominent commentator from *Mashable* to declare that "3D printers are never going to be a thing." Intrepid individuals who want to try their hand at 3D printing are nearly certain to experience a considerable amount of failure and are likely to be duly humbled as a result. We term this experience *"making failure"* and propose that, in addition to being humbling, this experience may also paradoxically lead to a sense of pride.

In other making contexts, failure often has more serious

consequences and is feared rather than celebrated. If an architect fails, a building could collapse. In contrast, 3D printing presents a low-risk setting in which failure is rarely consequential. If you did a Google search on the term "3D Printing Failure," you'd quickly learn two things: (1) Failure is quite common in the 3D printing realm, as this technology is far from plug and play, and (2) members of the desktop 3D printing community celebrate failures with a surprising degree of pride. For example, the Tumblr website Epic3Dprintingfail is a visual monument to 3D printing gone wrong. Makers proudly refer to their failures using terms such as "3D printing fail = learning," "things go delightfully askew," and "a thing of beauty!" Within the 3D printing community, failure appears to have little stigma. Instead, failure seems to have been normalized as part of the process of learning to become a maker. As noted by Richard Horne, who curates a Flickr gallery of 3D printing failures, "I've had a lot more failures than successes...You can learn a lot from failure."

Example of a 3D printing failure. So close, but so far away.

In order to put this proposition to the test, we studied *making failure* among members of the desktop 3D printing community. We conducted a survey among 190 members (across eleven different countries) of MyMiniFactory (MMF), one of the world's largest communities of 3D printing enthusiasts (www.myminifactory.com). With the help of the founders of MMF, we obtained access to its members, all of whom own desktop 3D printers and have used this new technology to make a wide variety of objects, such as repair parts, toys, and household objects. In our survey, we examined how the process of making a 3D printed object promotes a sense of humility. We also measured pride, by asking 3D printing enthusiasts to report their sense of accomplishment, confidence, and self-worth from engaging in 3D printing. Finally, we asked enthusiasts to report the degree to which they experienced making failure.

The results of our survey revealed a number of interesting insights. First, we found that 3D printing enthusiasts with higher levels of humility also demonstrated higher levels of pride. This positive association between humility and pride is an intriguing finding, as humility is often considered to be the antithesis of pride. However, as recently discovered by the psychologist Aaron Weidman and his colleagues, humility and pride may actually align under certain conditions.

Specifically, Weidman suggests that, "the notion that humility could follow a personal failure [...] is consistent with prior work suggesting that when people describe their experiences of humility, they often recall scenarios that follow a personal failure."[13] It appears that making objects via 3D printing is one of these conditions. Further investigation into our survey data revealed that the virtue of humility is strongest

13 Weidman, A. C., Cheng, J. T., & Tracy, J. L. (2018). The psychological structure of humility. *Journal of Personality and Social Psychology, 114*(1), 153.

among 3D printing enthusiasts who experienced the highest level of failure when engaging in the making process. This finding is somewhat expected, as failure is often viewed as a humbling experience.

However, because failing has become destigmatized by the 3D printing community, this humility is transformed into a sense of pride in the 3D printed object. In essence, failure appears to be both humbling and empowering at the same time. Enthusiasts who experience more failure are more humbled; in turn, this humility provides a sense of pride. Because of the destigmatization, 3D printing failures are not viewed as a personal shortcoming, but as part and parcel of engaging in this new technological realm.

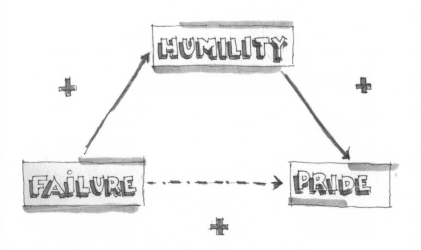

A deeper dive into our survey results revealed further insights regarding the characteristics of the 3D printing enthusiasts in our study and how these characteristics affect failure, humility, and pride:

1. Voice of Experience: Novices appear to be hurt by failure, but as they gain experience, failure becomes normalized. Our data revealed that 3D printing enthusiasts who were experts felt a greater degree of both humility and pride following *making failure* compared to novices. While novices may interpret failure as an indicator of their lack of competence, experts have the maturity to realize that failure happens, even to the best of us. The voice of experience helps us realize that failure is normal and that it can be both a source of pride as well as humility.

2. You are not Alone: Although we may fail, failing can lead to more positive outcomes when it occurs within a supportive community. Our research reveals that 3D printing enthusiasts who are part of an active online community such as MMF have the opportunity to share ideas and receive constructive feedback from others who share similar interests and experiences. As stated by one participant in our study, "I learn from my mistakes and I enter contests online so that I can learn what people like and don't like." As noted earlier, the 3D printing community has normalized failure so that this humbling experience is transformed into a sense of pride. In contrast, the positive association between humility and pride may be much less likely among individuals engaged in isolated acts of creation without the support of this type of community.

3D printing reality.

3. Equal Opportunity Employer: Making failure as a means of enhancing both humility and pride applies to nearly everyone, whether one lives in the US or China, is 18 or 77, lacks a high school diploma or holds a PhD. Given its recent emergence, desktop 3D printing is a technology that is relatively unfamiliar to most people. Thus, everyone faces a steep learning curve, regardless of location, gender, age, or education. As a result, failure appears to be commonplace among 3D printing enthusiasts from nearly all walks of life. The ubiquity of 3D printing failure likely plays an important role in normalizing setbacks and turning creations gone wrong into points of pride.

4. Passion not Profit: In contrast to companies, which make things for financial profit, 3D printing enthusiasts make things as a means of expressing their passions and interests. One of the participants in our study made a fidget spinner in which the arms mimic the shape of Donald Trump's hair, while another made a life-sized replica of a toy sword from their favorite video game. These types of idiosyncratic creations are commonplace in the desktop 3D printing community. Moreover, MMF is a file sharing website in which anyone in the world can download digital versions of these creations for free. Clearly, these enthusiasts are pursing passion rather than profits. As a result, failures during the making process are little more than minor annoyances. In

A 3D printed fidget spinner of Donald Trump's hair. Design created by Mirka Biel. *Posted on MyMiniFactory.*

contrast, when making fails in a corporate setting, the stakes are significantly higher.

5. Turn Ideas into Objects: The recent emergence of accessible and affordable desktop 3D printers gives nearly everyone the opportunity to turn their ideas into objects, in the comfort of their own homes. Without this technology, these ideas would likely remain only thoughts, hopes, and dreams. The opportunity to turn these ideas into actual objects that can be touched may be especially motivating despite the challenges posed by the current state of 3D printing technology. Hardships may make the outcome even more rewarding, as we tend to appreciate things that we work hard to achieve. One participant in our study noted, "I enjoy seeing new ideas… having something appear in reality that was just in your head can be life changing."

The importance of embracing failure is increasingly being recognized across a broad swath of domains including education, psychology, and business. Likewise, while there is growing interest in the ability of desktop 3D printing to create things we need, this emerging technology may also be a tool capable of shaping our sense of self by developing humility and pride in our work. Although failure humbles us, it may also create a sense of appreciation for the making process, which can also make us proud. In the end, the process of making is inherently rewarding regardless of whether your fidget spinner ends up looking like Donald Trump's hair or a hot mess.

At present, only a few million people own a desktop 3D printer. So the benefits of making failure through this technology are thus experienced by a relatively small portion of our population. Nonetheless, the growth rate is quite high and desktop 3D printers are increasingly popping up in a variety of publicly accessible venues such as makerspaces, libraries, and schools. In the near future, you will likely have the opportunity to enjoy the humbling pride of making failure via 3D printing yourself.

Inside the Illinois MakerLab at the University of Illinois at Urbana-Champaign.

HUMILITY VS.
HUMILIATION IN OLD AGE

Russell Belk

s I write this, my mother is ninety-seven. In the past three years, I have spent time with her in hospitals, nursing homes, and rehabilitation centers as she battled cancer and various other types of ill health. She has suffered physical pain and discomfort. But perhaps worse, she has suffered humiliation. Some of the humiliation comes from her infirmity, but some also comes from the actions of others. She makes younger others uncomfortable because she moves slowly, has a hard time hearing, takes time deciding, and doesn't always understand what she is told.

In turn, others make her uncomfortable because they are impatient, unsympathetic, annoyed, and intolerant. They assume that she is worse than the still sharp-minded and kind person that I know her to be. Even care personnel who regularly deal with the old and ill don't always respect the needs of the elderly for privacy, dignity, compassion, and respect. That my mother is humbled by her disabilities is understandable; that she is further humbled and humiliated by a disdainful society is not.

Humility is largely voluntary; humiliation is largely involuntary. Humility is a choice made with dignity. Humiliation is imposed from without as a result of callousness and prejudice. As we age there is often a natural tendency toward greater humility. We let go of vainglorious claims to status. We are freed from ambition. We can replace seeking to triumph over others with seeking to triumph over adversity. But if there is a greater chance for humility, there is also a greater threat of humiliation. Again, we must first make some personal allowance for and adjustments to our bodily limitations. After that it's a question of whether others we encounter will also make these accommodations. The question this raises is whether it is possible to age with humility, but without humiliation. Because of our potentially mellowed demeanor, we may well be perceived by others as more gentle, humble, and modest. But because of declines in our physical strength and mental agility as well as our youth, vigor, and skin tone, we may also be perceived by others as a stupid, ugly, and inferior annoyance. This is where humiliation comes in.

I am not talking about humiliation from the natural effects of aging which, in order to be humble, we should accept with grace. Age is a natural leveler and, as we become "senior citizens," we may be expected to let go of some of our pride, dispense with pretense, and redefine our identity as residing less in what we can do or what we have and more in our experience and wisdom. In later stages of life, we will be well served by overcoming our pride and adopting greater humility and perseverance. In doing so, we act to deflect or reduce others' temptation to humiliate us. A start in accomplishing this is to understand that they may well be reacting to us by projecting their own fears of aging and illness.

Next, we may need to shift our sense of self. When we retire, we can refer to our prior careers, jobs, and achievements, but as these accomplishments recede into the past, they are of less use in thinking about who we are right now. Instead we might look to our children, grandchildren, and great grandchildren and shift our pride to their accomplishments rather than our own. We may take vicarious pleasure in their triumphs and share vicarious pain in their setbacks, but it is less about us and more about them. If we own a vehicle, we are likely less desirous of a flashy sports car or high status marker than a vehicle that is easy to get in and out of and that is as automatic as possible. Eventually we will likely have to give up driving as well. In these and other ways, humility can grow naturally with age. We find new means to envision and express our identities in ways that may be less fashion-forward but that are nevertheless satisfying and rewarding. We can turn to long-delayed hobbies, interests, and reading without self-recriminations that we should be working or helping family. It is our turn to be waited upon.

Humiliation, on the other hand, may be felt in becoming dependent on others, having difficulty doing what we once did easily, embarrassing ourselves through incontinence, having to obey and defer to others instead of acting independently, and suffering potential ridicule due to degraded performance. We may also become financially dependent on others. As a result, we may grow lonely and alienated and lose the dignity we once enjoyed.

Michael Oliver and Susan Tureman both worked in a nursing home over a number of years. In a paper called "Discoveries" they describe nursing home residents as "beautiful, unpretentious human beings." They go on:

> They are forced into a presentation of self without the use of normal props. Makeup will not cover arthritic limbs, and legs requiring wheels inevitably force the drama to a lower level. But the more I interact with these persons, whose costumes give away the secrets of

the backstage, the more I admire their performances. They are real.

The passage evokes a combination of presentation of self and performance of self. Together, they suggest that old age is something that is performed, and it can involve a flawed presentation of self. For it involves performances without the benefits of all the sets, masks, and props that were a part of our living as thriving consumers during our younger years. Thus, we may be denied resources that could otherwise disguise our frailties or embellish our strengths.

Nevertheless, there is considerable opportunity to avoid humiliation through acting with dignity. Dictionary definitions of dignity stress that it is a personal trait and behavior rather than something bestowed by others. A typical definition states that it is the quality or state of being worthy of respect and honor. Others are more likely to bestow this respect and honor if we act with dignity. Respect begins with self-respect. This does not mean being haughty or acting as if we feel we are better than others. Rather it means being humble and respectful of the others whose respect we seek. In other words, when the elderly act with humility (but not deference) they are more likely to avoid humiliation. And for those who encounter the elderly, empathy, patience, and understanding can go a long way toward fostering mutual respect. In this respect we can learn something from Asian societies that respect the elderly to a much greater degree than most of us in the West.

The potential indignities of aging may be divided into three sets: those that are inherent in our biology, those that are structural, and those that are social. The biological set includes changes in our physical condition, mobility, skin condition, posture, muscle tone, and hair condition as well as forgetfulness, confusion, and technological bewilderment. Structural changes include loss of job, income, gift-giving ability, home, possessions, and vehicle, and perhaps loss of privacy within certain hospitals and nursing homes. The COVID-19 crisis in care homes has demonstrated limitations of relying upon underpaid and overworked caregivers, many of whom are immigrants to whom English is a second or third language. Stress, delays, and communication issues are hard to avoid under such circumstances. And those sources of indignity that are social include increased dependency on others, decline of attention by extended family, staff inattention, regimentation, disdain, and discourtesy. It is these latter social indignities that concern me the most. Biological and structural indignities are humbling, but social indignities are potentially unnecessary sources of humiliation.

Humor may be a way of overcoming some of these changes through self-mockery. But humor directed toward the elderly often reveals the presence of ageist mockery. This is shown in greeting cards that can become a vicious expression of ridicule and aggression. For example, one recent card showed an older couple with the woman looking in the mirror with concern. She says, "I feel horrible; I look old, fat and ugly. I really need you to pay me a compliment." Her partner replies, "Your eyesight's damn near perfect." Such negative messages (you are old, fat, and ugly) and stereotypes are not only prevalent in greeting cards, but also in film, television, advertising, and jokes. Targets of ridicule include declining mental abilities, unattractiveness, physical impairments, "old maids," bad health, provoking depression in others, impotence, and impending death. The old are depicted as being hard of hearing and having impaired eyesight and mobility. The stigma of aging is furthered by images of the elderly as disordered and dirty, repelling and repugnant. Furthermore, they are seen as incompetent and are, for example, assumed to be to blame in the case of automobile accidents. They are seen as old-fashioned, unproductive, and irrelevant.

But these are perceptions based on stereotypes. What matters more in terms of actually feeling humiliated are the ways in which the person is treated. Besides outright rejection in areas like employment, the elderly may be met with either benevolent or hostile ageism. Even benevolent ageism can be paternalistic, as when others use "elderspeak" consisting of exaggerated speech with overly simplified information and a demeaning emotional tone. Hostile ageism is characterized by a lack of warmth and ridicule, as may accompany what is perceived as age-inappropriate behavior by the elderly, such as liking contemporary music. These are behaviors and stereotypes that need to be countered by more age-positive images of the elderly in the media and in person. We are learning to challenge sexism and the same must be done with ageism.

Beleaguered health care workers cannot protect all residents from themselves and each other. Julia Neurberger describes life in a nursing home for one older man suffering physical and mental debilities after a vibrant life of self-assurance:

He was Jewish, very Orthodox, and gradually found himself unable to cope. He became incontinent, and on the hospital ward kept taking his clothes off. He never would have allowed anyone to see him naked if he had been himself, and it was extremely distressing for us to see him acting contrary to every rule he had lived by.

My mother recently was on the spectator end of such display, when a naked man walked into her room in her health care facility.

Similarly, Oliver and Tureman, the same couple who worked in a nursing home, reflected:

Mom will sleep with a stranger in her bedroom, she will eat food which is predetermined and served at specific times, she will be unable to take a bath when she wants one, and her bowel movements will be observed and monitored. If she gets upset, or raises her voice, she will be reprimanded. Finally, she will discover that parts of the home are "off-limits."

There is also a huge difference between more expensive facilities with private rooms and poorer facilities with four to a room separated only with bedsheet curtains. Those who can't afford a nursing home, in-home care, or palliative care in the case of debilitating fatal diseases have only family or homeless shelters to fall back on.

There are, of course, many other factors that shape the experience of aging including health, gender, ethnicity, religion, having a living partner, location, support networks, and private or social insurance. And if you live in a country without a public health care system, good luck. But cultural norms are also important. A Ghanaian colleague, Sammy Bonsu, and I found that in Ghana it was more honorable to use money to provide a loved one with a good funeral than it was to spend the money on drugs that might save their life or spare them pain. In much of Asia the old are revered, although the expectation of living out life with extended family is declining there as well. But one thing Asians tend to do in middle and old age is travel in groups, especially the Chinese. Urban Chinese also eat at restaurants in groups and share food at round tables with "lazy Susans" in the middle. In many Chinese cities older people also gather in the mornings or evenings to rhythmically exercise, dance, and do Tai Chi in groups. They help one another.

Similarly, until she was ninety-five, my mother was fortunate to live in a senior apartment complex where the residents really cared for and looked out for one another. While death is a common and accepted event in the complex, so is life. They enjoyed daily coffees and card games, a happy hour, and a weekly shared meal. While there, Mom was part of the group that was celebrated for being in their nineties. And she was proud to reflect on "Betty Belk Day" at her church, where her life story was summarized along with her role in helping found the church sixty-five years earlier. These little recognitions help to reinvigorate a type of modest pride that lives inside each of us as we begin to reflect on our lives. A simple act that we can all offer to bring about such moments is to ask and listen.

Death with dignity should be more than a motto for assisted suicide. Dignity can be elusive for both the poor and the rich. While the poor, women, minorities, and immigrants may suffer more hostile ageism, rich white men may have a more difficult time adjusting to the infirmities of aging after a lifetime of privilege. Likewise, despite being financially better off than the generations before and after them, the Baby Boom generation now entering old age may feel a greater shock after a lifetime of cultural dominance.

French writer, philosopher, and political activist Simone de Beauvoir observed that "the elderly person is marked as such by custom, by the behavior of others and by vocabulary itself." That is, the way others treat us tells us how old or infirm we are or are assumed to be. So does the vocabulary of the system that tells us we need a "handicapped sticker" when our only impairment is old age. Where we may have once appreciated when someone checked to determine whether we were old enough to legally buy alcohol, we may now wince when someone assumes that we should enjoy a senior citizen's discount. These are some of the many stigmas of aging. Religious ethicist Jane Foulcher compared the renunciations we make in old age to the practices of self-denial in a monastery: "Relinquishing ownership of worldly goods, celibacy, chastity, simplicity of life, and solitude."

But it doesn't have to be that way. In a less ageist society holding on, letting go, and enjoying our later years becomes more of a choice. Socially, we don't need to segregate the aged and keep them out of sight of others. France has a program in which university students can live free with elderly people who have room in their homes. In exchange the students are required to devote a certain number of hours per week to help the older person. But what inevitably happens is that a bond of friendship is formed, and no one counts hours. And these relationships often continue after the young person moves on. Getting old doesn't need to include the experiences that Foulcher found "of interminable waiting and monotonous routine, of destructive rumination and attendant distrust that too often characterize the lives of residents of aged care facilities."

Ultimately humiliation is a social construct. In a society of nudists, being nude in public is not a source of humiliation. In a society of enlightened, tolerant, and respectful people, the inevitable impairments of aging are not a source of stigma. And for someone who can afford care and services and who is fortunate enough to escape the most encumbering forms of physical and mental impairment, it is possible to largely avoid humiliation. For those who are less fortunate or less wealthy, such escape is impossible. Both society and individual caregivers need to work on removing negative bias toward the aged. Condescension breeds shame. Compassion breeds understanding. Fear of death is enough to face without the additional burden of humiliation.

as possibility

WHITENESS IS NEVER HUMBLE, EVEN WHEN IT IS

Tyler Denmead

1.
Humility has returned
in this moment
of unbridled
white arrogance. I
am ambivalent. Or,
I do not know how
to be but
ambivalent. Or,
I cannot pin down
who profits from
humility. Or,
I cannot pin down
who is
expended through
humility. Or,
I have never known
humility. I have
only known willful
ignorance.

2.
I went to private
school from 1982

to 1994. The
Academy. We were "In
Quest of the Best." I
liked being on
quests as long
as the quests weren't
too hard.
A graduate of
Yale, the grandfather
of a president, founded
the school. He
demanded pious
respect for
the past, the great
ages, the great
arrangements, the great
greats. We learned
what T.S. Eliot called
"the wisdom of
humility." I idoled
the football team
and their quiet
confidence, walking
from the locker
room onto the field with
straight faces and glaring
eyes, somber and slow, if
not casual, movements.
With this gesture
came centuries
of the undisturbed steady
spine, shoulders bracing the

burden of the metropole. But
this quiet confidence is
a quest under the
illusion of its own
stillness, always on the
move, projecting sacrifice,
projecting respect for
rules, for
the sake of the other
team. Like the
white colonizer, the quietly
confident never seeks
power for power's sake, but
for the betterment of the
colony and the colonized.

This quest, this
best. It is humble
and supremely
arrogant at the same
time. Not quite
there yet. But
entitled to be the best.
I guess there is no
quest, not really anyway,
when the best is
already guaranteed.
It is this contradiction
that gives humility
its profitability for me
and the quiet confidence.
Our futures are already

guaranteed so it is our
restraint in reframing this
future as a project, as
a quest,
that allows us to hold
ourselves in higher
esteem. Guaranteed
futures demand
arrogance, and yet,
it is our humility, when
confronted with
guarantees, that
explains (to us) why
we are up here, now,
again, winning. Without
the guarantee, humility
loses its profitability.
And this profitability
is not distributed evenly. It
is only as even as the
repetitions that keep
repeating into the
future. So when
I feel my spine
bracing, my face turning,
I feel this
project, this history,
this humility,
presenting itself to me as
a virtue in the form of an
embodied burden for
the sake of the other.

But I also know that
when my précis is
not short or clear enough,
when my shot is not straight
or true enough, when my dance
card is not long or full
enough, when my monuments
are not tall or stable enough,
when his kneeling is not
pious or quiet enough,
humility slips for
those who learned that
their future is already
guaranteed.
Shrill vanity and blithe
disregard for the unearned
nature of privilege screams
across the field in a
cheer cast in the
waning moments of
defeat. *That's alright.*
That's okay. You are
going to work for me
one day. Exhilarated,
freed from the burden of
composure, from the
burden of the metropole, from
the burden of humility
when humility was never
good enough for the setting
sun.

3.
Did you see what I just
did there? The self-criticism
as superiority? The preservation
through transformation? The
being vulnerable, the being
humble. The changing of the
rules and the rhetoric but
not much else? This move
to innocence is not available
to everyone, and this move
is a trap. It is one of
the traps we Academy boys
set for ourselves when we
perform the right side of
history, now, late,
performing humility. We locate
ourselves outside above and
beyond the strictures and
structures that still
replenish our pockets and
cover us with blood that is
never our own. I don't like this
trap, this trap that I have set
for myself. But there is so
little at stake here for me. This
trap isn't deadly at all. My
traps, they never
are.

MY JOURNEY FROM TECH SECTOR TO KITCHEN

Kevin Em

On a cold Monday morning in February, I was let go from a cybersecurity start-up without notice. Too proud to collect unemployment, sitting in a local café, I was desperate and walked across the shopping complex to the first restaurant I saw. I applied and was hired on the spot after pointing out a small line at the bottom of my resume noting that I had attended a cooking academy in Korea.

Getting put to work, another body in the machine, doing many things at the same time, and getting used to the grind was mind-numbing at first. After a dinner shift, I'd get this "face" where my mouth sagged down and I looked as if I may drop any second. But I got used to it and became less tired each week. I began to have a recurring dream that I had been found to be a fraud, a washout who slinks out the back of the restaurant to taunts of "you don't have what it takes, college boy!".

Being quick with my retorts was essential to getting along with the other cooks. I strained to focus on the banter and learned that my best assets were wit and polite deference. Soon my kitchen mates were helping me keep up with orders. It felt like being inducted abroad a pirate ship and I began to relish coming into work with misfits, sometimes alcoholics, and former drug addicts. You try timing the perfect profanity while using your "spidey sense" to avoid the clink of a dropped knife, grabbing red-hot sauté pans and sticking your arm in ovens bursting with flames to rescue half-burnt pizzas. It's demanding to cart a tower of dirty kitchenware past the entire line while avoiding towels snapping menacingly, tit-for-tat insults growing more outrageous.

I found the open kitchen liberating compared to the office of the tech company: the self-aggrandizing culture and supposedly flat organizational structure of start-ups, the requirement to have a one-page CV, and to be on call twenty-four/seven. At the restaurant, cooks ask where you're from. The rest is up to what you can do with your hands. And the shift ends at clock-out. In tech, a corporate boilerplate can take days to be approved by management (the phrase "too many cooks in the kitchen" is frequently used to describe this obsessing over minutiae). In the real kitchen, your own tasting spoon has the final word: if your soup sucks, you won't spend hours on a tri-continental video call until someone tells you it does.

This abrupt and invigorating change was not without pitfalls. I was disheartened by the extremely low wages of a line cook. I realized that I still felt the pull of the tech unicorn and craved brand name value. And I resolved to seek an employer that provided benefits in case the minor burns, bruises, blisters and brutalized lower back turned to bigger health problems. So, I applied to a temp position at the university hospital kitchen, thinking it would be more automated but the same outlet for my newfound passion.

Cooking in the B2 level of the hospital turned out to be grueling work. Some of our patients deal with chewing or swallowing disorders, so we'd evenly chop up chicken or whisk scrambled eggs to powder. Other customers were suicidal, so no silverware or bamboo skewers would be given on their trays. Cooking without salt, butter, or wine was a chore, but

I loved getting creative with it. And I enjoyed creating fragile, time-limited, and fragrant works of art on a hospital tray, never once seeing who ate the dish.

While I slowly gained confidence in cooking, I came to know my colleagues on the assembly line, shaped like the letter T, an engineering marvel in itself. The true force behind it all were the people—more than seven different languages being spoken at all times—who would kindly move out of your way while holding armfuls of salads, and always ask you how you're doing. The "old school" cooks wordlessly slide a cart next to you so it's easier to scoop soup out of the kettle. I liked the feeling of belonging, even among people who had worked the same positions, stored their things in the same locker, and showed up on time every day for decades.

In addition, I noted the stark parallels in inequalities that exist in B2 between chefs and doctors (white coats) and patient meal assembly and delivery staff (blue coats), though I found many of the blue-coated workers hold advanced degrees back in their home country. I learned that sometimes I have to step up to clean others' mistakes, no matter how unpleasant the task or whose fault it is. I resolved never to be late because my tardiness shortens another worker's break time. A cook takes time out to walk over and correct my knife-cleaning so it's not dirtier than before, or offers a simple tip to hold the bowl in my other hand to make it easier to ladle soup. Accepting feedback turns me into a better cook.

It's humbling to work with so many professionals, like Fe Victorio, a garde manger at the university hospital. She told me:

> Patience is the most important quality in the kitchen—
> you work with so many people of different cultures
> who communicate differently and believe different

things. You have to repeat yourself or change the way you express a request until the message gets across.

Arion Silmon, a chef's assistant at the hospital put his work this way:

> There are days where there's so much to do and you're constantly busy but once you go home and think back on all you've completed, you realize that you can accomplish a lot. You feel good about yourself after that rush.

The most humbling experience of my time in the hospital kitchen was when I was asked to cover for the dishwasher. In a matter of seconds, I was drenched head to toe after directing the high-powered nozzle into a spoon. I had not noticed the fan sitting in the corner, which I could have used to cool off in-between soaking each pan in soapy water, hot water, and sanitizer as trained. I became paranoid that I would be injured and forgotten in the dish room and started singing ditties like "row your boat" very loudly. Other cooks and food workers looked in with sympathetic eyes or knowing laughs when they dropped off cartloads of burnt mac and cheese or containers half-full of chicken noodle soup. It dawned on me: the most patient, humble, hard-working people on this earth are kitchen staff, most especially dishwashers.

Now each time I visit the dish tank with dirty pans, the "thank you's" come tumbling out. And I was excited to ask Ira J. Trussell, a dishwasher at the Hospital for an interview:

> I came to Michigan looking for a job and back then I had three choices, an auto plant, working for the city,

or at the hospital. When Ford, GM, Chrysler started laying people off, I didn't have enough seniority to get called back. I missed my interview with the city so I've been dishwashing at the hospital for thirty-two years. It's the steadiest job in the state and now, my age has caught up with me, I don't have the time to follow a company to another area. I learned to stretch my money and decided to stay in one place until God tells me I can't work anymore. I grew up on a farm in Alabama so I know what hard work means."

One morning during a huddle, or cooks' meeting, I noticed two Chinese women present, one translating for the other. I introduced myself in Mandarin and asked if they've had a meal or eaten, which is a proper greeting. They asked if I was Chinese and I answered "No, I'm Korean-American," and, gradually, my education came up. I told them of my graduate studies at Tsinghua University and having taken Chinese language courses at NYU. Their eyes lit up and one woman exclaimed, "What?? What are you doing working here?" and "What do your parents think? Are they okay with this??" The other woman quickly shushed her, then smiled at me.

I was intrigued by the prospect of cooking for and interacting with thousands of undergraduate students each day and my colleagues urged me to apply for an on-campus position, which they said would be a better match for my temperament and goals as a cook. Before my scheduled interview and practical test to be a cook at Mosher-Jordan residence hall, my colleagues gave me ample tips on what to expect on the test and gifted me a giant box-cutter to break down the many boxes I'd process when receiving food shipments in the dining hall. Echoes of good luck reverberated through the halls as I clocked out for the last time at the university hospital.

In Mosher-Jordan, the first question of the practical test immediately stumped me. I thought to myself: what the hell is a *roux*? The recipe given called for adding it to my vegetable chowder. I dutifully weighed the seasonings and finely diced the produce, and even mopped my station before doubling back to the first step, which held that mysterious word I had never seen before. I poked around the corner of the kitchen and approached a nearby cook.

"Excuse me sir, I know I shouldn't be asking during a test, but could you kindly tell me what this "*rooks*" is here at the top of the recipe?" I said breathlessly.

"Oh, you mean a 'roo'? Come here, let me show you." He paused what he was doing and walked over to the stove. "What we'll need is another pot," as he bent to grab another rondeau pan. And slowly, methodically, this cook named David showed me how to add a roux to thicken my first chowder. He quietly left to finish up his task, while I turned off the heat and searched for chef for the tasting. To my surprise, five more cooks appeared each holding their own spoon. Their spoons plunged into the chowder.

The first said, "I like that he used another pan for roux. And look, it all fits on a spoon."

Another blew, slurped, and gruffed, "Certainly edible."

There was appreciative mumbling all around. I felt elated.

"Well Kevin," said chef, "I think it's unanimous that we'd love to have you with us."

CONTRIBUTORS

Aaron Ahuvia is a Professor of Marketing at the University of Michigan-Dearborn whose work literally focuses on peace, love, and happiness. Regarding happiness, he has published extensively on how our lives as consumers—earning and spending money—influence our psychological well-being. Regarding love, he is the leading authority on why we love objects and activities, as well as how our love for our favorite things relates to the love we have for people. Finally, with regard to peace, his expertise includes training people to better understand others who are different from them. This is important to businesses that need to understand their customers. But he has also used his expertise to work with organizations promoting peaceful conflict resolution. Currently, he works with Better Angels, an organization seeking to reduce polarization between liberals and conservatives. A published study ranked him 22nd in the world for research influence in consumer behavior. He has been quoted in *Time*, *The Wall Street Journal*, *The New York Times*, and has appeared on NPR and television shows such as *The Oprah Winfrey Show*.

Russell Belk is Kraft Foods Canada Chair in Marketing and York University Distinguished Research Professor. His current research involves sharing, digital consumption, gift-giving, and consumption of technology. This work tends to be qualitative, visual, and cultural. He has received the Paul D. Converse Award, two Fulbright Awards, and the Sheth Foundation/ Journal of Consumer Research Award for Long

Term Contribution to Consumer Research. He is a fellow in the Royal Society of Canada, the Association for Consumer Research, and the American Psychological Association. He has more than 700 publications in print and film. His writing has been cited more than 75,000 times. Together with colleagues he initiated the Consumer Behavior Odyssey, the Association for Consumer Research Film Festival, and the Consumer Culture Theory Conference.

Charles M. Blow is an Op-Ed columnist at *The New York Times*. His columns tackle hot-button issues such as social justices, racial equality, presidential politics, police violence, gun control, and the Black Lives Matter Movement. Mr. Blow is also a CNN commentator and a Presidential Visiting Professor at Yale, where he teaches a seminar on media and politics. He is the author of the critically acclaimed *New York Times* bestselling memoir, *Fire Shut Up in My Bones*. The book won a Lambda Literary Award and the Sperber Prize and made multiple prominent lists of best books published in 2014. *People* magazine called it "searing and unforgettable." Mr. Blow joined *The New York Times* in 1994 as a graphics editor and quickly became the paper's graphics director, a position he held for nine years. Mr. Blow went on to become the paper's design director for news before leaving in 2006 to become the art director of *National Geographic Magazine*. Before coming to the *Times*, Mr. Blow had worked at *The Detroit News*. Mr. Blow graduated magna cum laude from Grambling State University in Louisiana, where he received a B.A. in mass communications, and he holds an honorary doctorate from Massachusetts College of Art and Design in Boston.

Richard C. Boothman, JD served as the Chief Risk Officer at the University of Michigan Health System for seventeen years and is an adjunct Assistant Professor in the Department of Surgery at the UM Medical School and Visiting Scholar, Vanderbilt University Medical Center, Center for Patient and Professional Advocacy. He led development of the "Michigan Model," a proactive response to patient injury founded on honesty and transparency. The Michigan Model has garnered national and international attention for reducing malpractice costs while improving patient safety. Boothman's work has been featured on National Public Radio's *Weekend Edition*, *All Things Considered,* and *Marketplace*, the New England Journal of Medicine, CBS News, CNN, MSNBC, *The New York Times*, the *Wall Street Journal*, BBC radio, and the Korean Broadcasting System among many others.

Ruth Nicole Brown is an artist-scholar whose life work is dedicated to the celebration of Black girlhood. The Inaugural Chairperson of African American and African Studies at Michigan State University, her study of Black girlhood emerges from over a decade of practice—face to face conversations, rituals of dance and movement, and active relationship building with Black girls and women in Saving Our Lives Hear Our Truths, which is lovingly referred to by the acronym SOLHOT. Author of *Black Girlhood Celebration: Toward A Hip-Hop Feminist Pedagogy* and *Hear Our Truths: The Creative Potential of Black Girlhood*, Ruth Nicole was awarded the Whiting Public Engagement Fellowship for SOLHOT's premier project, Black Girl Genius Week.

Sarah Buss is a Professor in the Department of Philosophy at the University of Michigan. Professor Buss is interested in issues at the intersections of ethics, moral psychology, and action theory. She is the author of articles on autonomy, moral responsibility, practical rationality, and respect for persons. In her work, she has developed accounts of weakness of will, our moral obligations to the needy, the rationality of our concern for our own happiness, the relationship between intentional action and evaluative commitments, the relevance of childhood deprivation to assignments of blame, the moral importance of etiquette, and the metaphysical significance of illness. Her current projects address the normative significance of formal principles of practical rationality, the nature of reasons for action, the will's contribution to action, and the moral implications of certain basic human capacities.

Agnes Callard is Associate Professor of Philosophy and Director of Undergraduate Studies at the University of Chicago. She received her MA in Classics, and her PhD in Philosophy, both from UC Berkeley. She has just written a book titled *Aspiration: The Agency of Becoming*, which offers an account of how we work to acquire new values. In the book, she argues that value-acquisition should be understood as a learning process, and thus that there is a distinctively practical form of learning. She also works in ancient philosophy, having written articles on Plato's *Protagoras*, *Gorgias*, *Hippias Minor* and *Meno*, and on Aristotle's *Nicomachean Ethics*.

Lynette Clemetson is a longtime journalist who loves helping reporters do their best work. She's worked in print, in digital, in magazines, newspapers, and radio, in the field and as a manager. As director of the Knight-Wallace Fellowships for Journalists and the Livingston Awards at the University of Michigan, she works to develop the careers of accomplished journalists from around the world who work in every medium on every platform. A former reporter for *Newsweek* and *The New York Times* and a former manager at NPR, she is a fierce defender of press freedom. She believes there is an incredible amount of important, impactful, innovative reporting being done now...if only people (herself included) could stop scrolling long enough to absorb more of it.

Nadia Danienta is a Ph.D. candidate in Marketing at the University of Illinois at Urbana-Champaign specializing in consumer behavior research. Her research focuses on topics related to identity, specifically how artificial intelligence changes our identity and subsequent behavior. Prior to the doctoral program, Nadia received her B.S. in Biopsychology, Cognition, and Neuroscience and her M.S. in Psychology from the University of Michigan in Ann Arbor. Nadia has played the violin for over ten years and the process of learning it (with many mistakes) has been a humbling process.

Tyler Denmead teaches in the Faculty of Education and Queens' College at the University of Cambridge. He is the author of *The Creative Underclass: Youth, Race, and the Gentrifying City* (Duke University Press, 2019).

Mickey Duzyj is an artist and director known for his innovative use of animation in documentary film. He was chosen by *Variety* magazine as one of 2019's "Top 10 Documentary Filmmakers to Watch" and is the creator/director of the critically-acclaimed Netflix documentary series *Losers* (2019). He lives in upstate New York with his wife and two boys.

Kevin Em is a writer and cook at the University of Michigan. His writing explores Korean-American identity, migrant stories, and the concept of work based on his kitchen experience. Previously, he worked as a marketing manager in the tech industry. He received his B.A. in English from New York University and an M.A. in International Relations from Tsinghua University.

Kevin Hamilton has now lived longer in his current home of Urbana, Illinois than he lived in his birthplace of Greenville, South Carolina. Though for some years in between he pursued studies in other parts of the United States, his roots are now deep in the soil once called home by the Peoria, Kaskaskia, Miami, and a host of other native nations. Originally trained as a painter and public artist, Kevin has published on such topics as racial bias in algorithmic systems, methods of interdisciplinary collaboration, and photography's role in nuclear weapons development and policy. Among his other commitments are service as a teacher in a local LGBTQ-affirming church congregation and life as the father of two children. He is currently Dean of the College of Fine and Applied Arts at the University of Illinois, Urbana-Champaign.

Eranda Jayawickreme is Associate Professor of Psychology and Senior Research Fellow at the Program for Leadership and Character at Wake Forest University. His research focuses on well-being, moral psychology, psychological growth following adversity, wisdom, and integrative theories of personality, and has worked with populations in Rwanda, Sri Lanka, and various populations in the USA. His awards include the 2015 Rising Star award from the Association for Psychological Science, a Mellon Refugee Initiative Fund Fellowship, and grants from the John Templeton Foundation, the Templeton Religion Trust, the Templeton World Charity Foundation, the European Association for Personality Psychology, and the Asia Foundation/USAID. His work has been featured in publications such as *The New York Times* and *Slate*.

Troy Jollimore's most recent collection of poetry, *Syllabus of Errors*, was chosen by *The New York Times* as one of the best poetry books of 2015. His previous poetry books are *At Lake Scugog* (2011) and *Tom Thomson in Purgatory*, which won the National Book Critics Circle Award in poetry for 2006. His fourth poetry collection, *Earthly Delights*, will be published by Princeton in 2021. He is also the author of two philosophical works, *Love's Vision* and *On Loyalty*, and has received fellowships from the Bread Loaf Writers Conference, the Stanford Humanities Center, and the Guggenheim Foundation. His prose writings have appeared in *Conjunctions,* the *Kenyon Review, The New York Times Book Review, Midwest Studies in Philosophy,* the *American Philosophical Quarterly,* and elsewhere.

Melissa Koenig is Professor of Child Psychology at the Institute of Child Development at the University of Minnesota. Her research lies at the intersection of cognitive development and social understanding, and centers on how testimony functions as a source of knowledge. She directs the Early Language and Experience Laboratory and their work is published in journals including *Perspectives of Psychological Science, Psychological Science*, and the *Proceedings of the National Academy of Sciences*. She is President-Elect of the Cognitive Development Society and Fellow of the Association for Psychological Science. Her work has been funded by the National Institutes of Health, the National Science Foundation, and the John T. Templeton Foundation.

Rebekah Modrak is a writer and artist whose interventionist artworks resist consumer culture. *Re Made Co.* (remadeco. org) poses as an online "company" promoting $350 artisanal toilet plungers to parody actual company Best Made Co., seller of $350 luxury hand-painted axes. RETHINK SHINOLA (rethinkshinola.com) guides viewers through the Shinola company's past and present of marketing White supremacy. You can read her thoughts about culture jamming and reclaiming meaning from brand rhetoric in *The Routledge Companion to Criticality in Art, Architecture and Design*, *Afterimage*, *Consumption Markets & Culture*, *Ms. Magazine*, *The Conversation*, and *Infinite Mile*. She is a professor in the Stamps School of Art & Design at the University of Michigan.

Aric Rindfleisch is the John M. Jones Professor of Marketing and Executive Director of the Illinois MakerLab at the University of Illinois. Aric's research focuses on consumers and brands, interfirm relationships, and new product development and has been published in several leading academic journals including the *Journal of Marketing*, *Journal of Marketing Research*, *Journal of Consumer Research*, *Journal of Operations Management*, and *Strategic Management Journal*. His research has been cited by the *Chicago Tribune*, *The New York Times*, and the *Huffington Post*. Aric is also an award-winning teacher and was named by Princeton Review as one of the Best 300 Professors in America. He also teaches three popular Coursera classes (Marketing in a Digital World, Marketing in an Analog World & The 3D Printing Revolution). Aric built his first 3D printer in 2010 and enjoys making things that can't be bought in a store.

Gilbert B. Rodman has been teaching and writing about media, race, and culture for most of his adult life. He's the author of *Why Cultural Studies?* (Wiley Blackwell, 2015) and *Elvis After Elvis* (Routledge, 1996), the editor of *The Race and Media Reader* (Routledge, 2014), and co-editor of *Race in Cyberspace* (Routledge, 2000). He'd be happy to stop doing all that, but since the world seems all too eager to keep racism alive and well, he continues to have plenty of fresh problems to teach and write about. Buy him a beer and ask nicely (or maybe even just ask nicely), and he'll tell you more than you probably want to know about his current project on race and copyright, and why the world would probably be a better place if we rethought the whole notion of copyright from the ground up. He's currently Associate Professor of Communication Studies at the University of Minnesota.

Valerie Tiberius is a philosopher who likes to write about well-being and virtue. She also tries to find some of them in her own life, and she is helped in this effort by family, friends, singing, biking, and her dogs Sugar and Olive. She is the author of *The Reflective Life: Living Wisely With Our Limits* (Oxford, 2008), *Moral Psychology: A Contemporary Introduction* (Routledge, 2015), and *Well-Being as Value Fulfillment: How We Can Help Each Other to Live Well* (Oxford, 2018). She is currently the Paul W. Frenzel Chair in Liberal Arts and professor of philosophy at the Department at the University of Minnesota.

Jamie Vander Broek is an art librarian at the University of Michigan. She buys all kinds of art and design and artists' books for her library and runs a book arts studio where you can learn to print with metal type and make books by hand. A few years ago, she bought a book made of cheese for her library.

You can read her essay about it on saveur.com. She holds a tailored Master's degree from the U-M School of Information in Art and Art Museum Librarianship, and received a B.A. in Art History with a minor in Italian Studies from Wellesley College. Since arriving in Ann Arbor, she has been active in the local art and book communities, and is currently on the board of the Ann Arbor District Library. She lives in a constantly under-construction house with her husband, daughter, and two out-of-control Miniature Australian Shepherds.

In 2012, **Ami Walsh** co-founded an audio storytelling program for hospitalized patients with the Gifts of Art Program at Michigan Medicine's University Hospital. She is a graduate of the MFA Program for Writers at Warren Wilson College and her creative writing has received support from the Banff Arts Centre, Ox-Bow School of Art, the Ragdale Foundation, and the Vermont Studio Center. She currently works at the medical specialty camp North Star Reach, where, among her many duties, she directs an audio storytelling program for children with serious illnesses and their family members.

Jeremy Wood was not born humble, and he did not achieve humility through profound empathy and a principled commitment to human equality or environmental stewardship. Rather, he's from the "had humility thrust upon him" school of moral improvement. Notwithstanding a privileged upbringing and an elite education which included a PhD in political psychology from the University of Michigan, Jeremy is chronically unemployed. Practically forced to try entrepreneurship, Jeremy has achieved there a humility-inspiring record. IRBtool (an interactive guide to regulations designed to protect human subjects) achieved $0 in revenues.

Jeremy earned a patent for a method of protecting privacy in location data, but he is not even the best known "Jeremy Wood" in that field, and, again, his innovation earned $0 in revenues. Jeremy helped launch a private, bilingual school which enrolled 160 students before he was forced to relinquish ownership of this money-losing operation. Fortunately, Jeremy is well-medicated, his wife loves him, he's managed to convince his children that he's a success, and, if you are reading this, he's recognized as an expert on humility.

Jennifer Cole Wright is Professor of Psychology at the College of Charleston, USA. Her area of research is moral development and moral psychology more generally. She is interested in how moral values and norms develop over time and influence people's reactions to divergent beliefs and practices in pluralistic societies—and, in particular, the influence of individual and social "liberal vs. conservative" mindsets on those reactions. She is also interested in why we care about being "good people" and how we become them. In particular, she studies humility and the development of virtue, as well as young children's early moral development. She has published papers on these and other topics in journals like *Cognition, Mind and Language, Journal of British Developmental Psychology, Journal of Experimental Social Psychology, Journal of Moral Education, Philosophical Psychology, Journal of Cognition and Culture, Personality and Individual Differences, Social Development, Personality and Social Psychology Bulletin,* and *Merrill-Palmer Quarterly.* She has published a book, *Understanding Virtue: Theory and Measurement,* with Nancy Snow and Michael Warren (Oxford, 2020), and edited two interdisciplinary volumes: *Humility* (Oxford, 2019) and *Advances in Experimental Moral Psychology* (co-edited with

Hagop Sarkissian; Bloomsbury, 2014). When she's not writing, she is usually busy warping young minds in the classroom, trekking (often with students) across Europe, Southeast Asia, or East Africa—or sometimes just off on an adventure (with the help of a fuel-efficient car) across the US.

ACKNOWLEDGEMENTS

This project evolved over three years, and many people contributed to its growth from an idea that Rebekah carried back with her from Nebraska to the book you now hold in your hands.

Philosopher Sarah Buss, who wrote the brilliant introduction, and marketing professor Aaron Ahuvia were part of our original group of four. We first came together over the course of a year to plan a weekend of conversations investigating the role of humility in our contemporary lives. drawing inspiration from the academic halls of philosophy and consumer culture, the prep boards of cooks, the notebooks of journalists, and the fields of farming. Generous funding by Mcubed, a campus-wide seed funding program at the University of Michigan, supported this early action.

We thank all the contributors and collaborators who helped translate the intimacy of this first small event into the expansiveness of shared stories for this collection.

Graduate and undergraduate students at the university—Carolyn Gennari, Sarah Posner, and Maggie Johnson—facilitated a smooth event in October 2017, and Marjorie Gaber, Ana Vincent, Mara Ezekiel, and Tori Essex, along with professor and artist Nick Tobier, drew throughout the series of talks to express these imaginings and accounts through imagery as well as written word.

Thank you to Nick for thoughtfully following essays as they evolved over the course of time, and for creating the compelling, whimsical artworks that accompany each essay in this book to ensure that intelligences are visual as well as textual. Thank you to designers Sam Oliver and Joe Iovino for creating a look, feel, and home for the project on the web that invites readers to slow down and take time processing complex insights about humility. An additional thank you to Joe for his beautiful watercolor illustrations of each contributor. We are grateful to Ben Denzer for creating the perfect cover design.

This collection of essays owes an enormous debt to poet and literary translator Mike Zhai, our independent editor from midway into the writing process to the final engaging essays you read in the book. Whether the essay's subject was psychology, aging, or maker culture, Mike's brilliant observations, questions, and references pushed us all to consider our work from new perspectives. We are thankful for his guidance.

Many other people read the essays over their years of development, and noted thanks to Mary-Catherine Harrison, in the final push, and to Sarah Buss for taking time out of busy schedules and giving each of us substantial commentary to make our writing stronger.

Fauzia Burke was an early champion of this work and its necessity in our current political and cultural climate. Thank you, Fauzia, for shepherding us through the process of connecting with audiences curious about these ideas. With our appreciation for and wariness about social media, we're grateful that Rey Jeong became our companion in looking for stories related to humility in a sea of the opposite. Thank you, Amy Hughes, for advice and conversation about publishing.

You are only reading this collection because Anne Trubek is a rare publisher who values the essay collection as a way of exploring varied and previously unheard voices. Thank you, Anne for your intellectual curiosity, for taking a chance on a cold email from Rebekah, for making all of these contributors our companions in conversation, and for enthusiastically bringing this project into the world of your rocking, midwestern operation, the perfect home for our book. Anne led us to our talented and lightning fast editor, Martha Bayne, who notices the detail and the big picture.

Throughout the process of creating this book, we were supported by our home institutions at the University of Michigan: the Penny W. Stamps School of Art & Design and the University of Michigan Library.

Finally, we must thank our families and friends most especially for listening to us talk about humility and this project for three years. A special thank you to Nick, Lucy, Oscar, Bob, and Fran, and to Izaak, Ottilie, Meredith, Emily, Meghan, and Heidi. We love you all!

—*Rebekah Modrak and Jamie Vander Broek*